Practical Ideas
That Really Work
for Students with
Disruptive, Defiant, or Difficult Behaviors

Practical Ideas
That Really Work
for Students with
Disruptive, Defiant, or Difficult Behaviors

Preschool through Grade 4

Kathleen McConnell

Gail Ryser

James R. Patton

An International Publisher

8700 Shoal Creek Boulevard
Austin, Texas 78757-6897
800/897-3202   Fax 800/397-7633
www.proedinc.com

© 2002 by PRO-ED, Inc.
8700 Shoal Creek Boulevard
Austin, Texas 78757-6897
800/897-3202   Fax 800/397-7633
www.proedinc.com

ISBN-13: 978-0-89079-893-5

Printed in the United States of America

5   6   7   8   9   10   11   12   13   14   16   15   14   13   12   11   10   09   08   07

Contents

Introduction

We created this book, *Practical Ideas That Really Work for Students with Disruptive, Defiant, or Difficult Behaviors* for educators and other school-based professionals who work with students who display an array of challenging behaviors. This resource provides an assessment system and set of intervention ideas for students whose behaviors are

- Disruptive (they exhibit acting out behaviors),

- Defiant (they have difficulty with compliance in the classroom), or

- Difficult (they have poor peer relationships or have emotional adjustment problems that interfere with their ability to learn).

The overall intent is to offer teachers a resource that is easy to use and full of practical intervention ideas.

The materials in this book are intended for use with students in preschool through grade 4. A second book of practical ideas for *older* students with disruptive, defiant, and difficult behaviors is available in this series and is intended for use with students in grades 5 through 12. The general approaches and philosophy in the two books are the same; however, the forms that accompany the practical ideas in this version for younger students include many pictures and require little reading ability. The forms in the version for older students are more sophisticated and require some reading. Teachers of students in grades 4 or 5 may want to examine both volumes and select the book that best fits the maturity and reading level of their students.

Components

Practical Ideas That Really Work for Students with Disruptive, Defiant, or Difficult Behaviors includes two main components.

An **evaluation form** *with a rating scale, intervention plan, and ideas matrix.* The rating scale portion of the evaluation form is a criterion-referenced measure for evaluating problem behaviors that impact student learning. Teachers rate a student on a list of behaviors, and, based on the rating, choose two or three behaviors to target for intervention. The intervention plan, provided in the evaluation form, offers teachers a way to

- document the behaviors they are targeting for intervention,

- indicate the specific intervention ideas they are implementing,

- note the starting date of the intervention, and

- make some notes concerning the effectiveness of the intervention.

The ideas matrix on the evaluation form provides a systematic way of linking the results of the rating scale to interventions. We hope that educators use the matrix as a tool for selecting effective interventions to meet each student's specific needs.

A teacher-friendly **resource manual** *of practical ideas.* The ideas were written to assist teachers and other school-based professionals in improving students' positive behaviors and decreasing their challenging behaviors. The book contains a short explanation of each idea, along with reproducible worksheets, examples, illustrations, and tips designed for easy implementation. The book also includes two appendixes. Appendix A is a blackline master of the Intervention Plan form that may be reproduced if additional copies are needed. Appendix B contains icons that can be used to customize many of the forms that accompany the practical ideas.

Development of the Behavior Problems Rating Scale

The criterion-referenced Rating Scale is designed for use by teachers or other school-based professionals to rate a student's behavior problems. The measure was designed to assist teachers in conducting a careful and thorough assessment of the specific behavior problems in four major areas that leads to the selection of intervention strategies.

Item Development

In order to address the behaviors most relevant to educators, we consulted several sources when selecting items for this scale. While there is no single definition or classification system that addresses all the behavior concerns in schools, we considered items from several sources. First, we included items that relate to the federal definition of serious emotional disturbance, since this disability category is most closely related to students' behavior problems. Second, we included items that are descriptive of many of the diagnostic criteria for Oppositional Defiant Disorder or Conduct Disorder listed in the *Diagnostic and Statistical Manual of Mental Disorders–Fourth Edition–Text Revision* (DSM–IV–TR; American Psychiatric Association, 2000) because students with these two diagnoses often experience behavioral difficulties in school. Finally, we included items describing problem behaviors most frequently cited in the research (The Sixth Phi Delta Kappa Poll of Teachers' Attitudes Toward the Public School, 2000), since these include behaviors of greatest concern to teachers. This scale is *not* intended to be used to diagnose any of these disorders; rather it is intended as a tool for determining intervention strategies and writing IEP goals and objectives.

The resulting measure consists of 40 items; 10 items in each of the four areas: acting out/serious misconduct, noncompliance in the classroom, poor peer relationships, and emotional adjustment problems. While most of the ideas in this book address the first three areas, we also included emotional adjustment problems because an increasing number of students in schools today exhibit symptoms of depression, anxiety, and other mental health problems. We hope that the inclusion of items related to emotional adjustment will help teachers increase their awareness of these problems and provide help for addressing them. However, we acknowledge the fact that teachers are not counselors or psychologists. It is imperative that teachers alert appropriate school personnel such as the school counselor or school psychologist if a student is rated high in the emotional adjustment problems area.

Responses to the items in the scale are based on a 5-point Likert system, with 0 meaning the student never exhibits the behavior and 4 meaning the student consistently exhibits the behavior to the point that it almost always is a problem. Items receiving a rating of 3 or 4 indicate that the behavior is a problem and is likely to be adversely affecting educational performance. These are the behaviors the teacher should target for immediate intervention.

Field Testing the Rating Scale

The criterion-referenced measure was field tested in three school districts in Texas with 118 students. Sixty-two of these students were identified as having a serious emotional disturbance (SED) or a behavioral disorder. The other 56 students had no diagnosis or a diagnosis of a learning disability. The original sample of 118 students was divided into two groups. Group 1 consisted of students 5 to 10 years of age and Group 2 consisted of students 11 through 18 years of age. For the analyses described in this book, intended for use with younger students, we used only the 44 students in Group 1 (ages 5 to 10).

Twenty-one of the 44 students were identified with an SED or a behavioral disorder and 23 had no diagnosis. Thirty of these young students were male (18 with an emotional or behavioral disorder; 12 with no diagnosis). Fourteen students were female (3 with an emotional or behvarioal disorder; 11 with no diagnosis). All students were in preschool through grade 4.

An item analysis was conducted using this sample. The resulting reliability coefficients were .97 for Acting Out/Serious Misconduct, .96 for Noncompliance in the Classroom, .95 for Poor Peer Relationships, and .95 for Emotional Adjustment Problems. The magnitude of these coefficients strongly suggests that the rating scale possesses little test error and that users can have confidence in its results.

In addition, we compared the mean ratings of the four subscales for the two groups, students identified with an emotional or a behavioral disorder and students without a diagnosis, using a *t* ratio. Our hypothesis was that students identified with SED or a behavior disorder would be rated higher than students with neither of these conditions. Because we made four comparisons for each group, we used the Bonferroni method to adjust the alpha level and set the alpha at .01. In each case the mean differences between the two groups were large enough to support our hypothesis. The probability in all cases was < .001. We can conclude that the rating scale is sensitive enough to discriminate between the two groups.

Development of the Practical Idea Manual

Teachers and other school-based personnel have many responsibilities and duties as part of their role in schools. In our discussions with teachers, supervisors, and counselors about the development of this product, they consistently emphasized the need for materials that are practical, easy to implement in the classroom, and not overly time consuming. We appreciated their input and worked hard to meet their criteria as we developed the ideas in this book. In addition, we conducted an extensive review of the literature and stayed focused on ideas supported by data documenting their effectiveness. The result is a book with

34 ideas, most with reproducible masters, and all grounded in our research and collective experience as well as that of the many educators who advised us and shared information with us. Our overriding orientation is to provide interventions that use positive behavioral strategies. However, we have included a few ideas intended to reduce challenging behaviors.

Assessment often provides much useful information to educators about the strengths and deficits of students. However, unless the information gathered during the assessment process affects instruction, its usefulness for school-based staff is limited. With this in mind, we designed an ideas matrix (see the Evaluation Form) so that educators can make the direct link between the data generated by the rating scale and classroom-focused instruction. We believe that this format conforms to our intention of providing information that is practical and useful.

Directions for Using the Materials

Step 1: Collecting Student Information

The first step is to complete the first page of the Evaluation Form for the child who exhibits disruptive, defiant, or difficult behaviors. As an example, Randi's completed Evaluation Form is provided in Figure 1. Space is provided on the front of the form for pertinent information about the student being rated, including name, birth date, age, school, grade, rater, and educational setting. In addition, the dates the student is observed and the amount of time the rater spends with the student can be recorded here. Also included on the front of the form is space to record the student's behavior problems that are of most concern to the teacher and the interventions that have previously been implemented.

Step 2: Rate the Behaviors of the Student

Pages 2 and 3 of the Evaluation Form contain the Rating Scale. The items are divided into the four areas discussed previously. Instructions for administering and scoring the items are provided on the form. Space is also provided to check the items to target for immediate intervention; that is, those items receiving a 3 or 4.

Step 3: Generate an Intervention Plan

Page 4 of the Evaluation Form contains the Intervention Plan. This section provides the examiner with space to record the target behaviors for intervention, the ideas for intervention, the starting date, and information relating to the effectiveness of the intervention.

Pages 5 and 6 of the Evaluation Form contain the Ideas Matrix, which should be consulted when completing the Intervention Plan. After choosing the problems to target for immediate intervention, the professional should turn to the Ideas Matrix and select an intervention that corresponds to that problem. The professional should then write the idea number and the starting date on the space provided on the Intervention Plan.

For example, Randi received the highest ratings in one area of Acting Out/Serious Misconduct (Item 8, Avoids accepting responsibility for own behavior) and two areas of Noncompliance in the Classroom (Item 7, Fails to follow classroom rules and procedures; and Item 10, Disrupts teaching and learning). Her teacher has targeted these three behaviors and has chosen Ideas 3, 22, 32, 13, and 7 from the Ideas Matrix. Because the area of major concern is "disrupts teaching and learning," the teacher will begin with Ideas 3 and 22 on January 15, 2002.

Step 4: Read and Review the Practical Ideas That Have Been Selected

The teacher should read the one-page explanation for each idea selected in Step 3. To aid in implementation, most of the ideas have at least one reproducible form on the page(s) following the explanation. A small icon in the top right-hand corner of the idea page indicates an accompanying form. Some ideas did not lend themselves to a reproducible form but are supported with explanations, suggestions for use, illustrations, tips, resource lists, and boxes of further information. Ideally, the teacher or other professional should also decide how and when to evaluate the effectiveness of each intervention. In our example with Randi, this could be accomplished by recording the number of times she disrupts teaching and learning during a 3- to 4-week period before intervening.

Step 5: Implement the Idea

After the teacher is familiar with the idea and has prepared all necessary materials, implementation can begin. The practical ideas selected for implementation can easily be integrated into an overall instructional design that reflects good instructional practices in the classroom.

Step 6: Evaluate the Effectiveness of the Practical Idea

After the intervention has been implemented for a reasonable amount of time (usually 3 to 6 weeks), the teacher should determine whether it is working. This can be done by evaluating relevant behavioral data related to the frequency, duration, or severity of the behaviors identified from the assessment. If the intervention is successful, the teacher can move on to the next problem. Sometimes the same idea can be used to target different behaviors. In our example, Randi's teacher will use Idea 3, Ask Me About My Day, to reduce the number of times Randi disrupts teaching and learning and to increase the degree to which Randi follows classroom rules.

References

American Psychiatric Association. (2000). *Diagnostic and statistical manual of mental disorders–Fourth edition–Text revision.* Washington, DC: Author.

Langdon, C. A., & Vesper, N. (2000). The sixth Phi Delta Kappa poll of teachers' attitudes toward the public schools [Electronic Version]. *Kappan, 81*(8), 607–611.

Research Supporting the Practical Ideas

This section provides references that have supporting data for the practical ideas in the book. These references should provide interested professionals with relevant information, should they wish to learn more about the interventions we have described. We have grouped the references by general category, according to our focus during our research.

Building Positive Relationships

Clark, H. B., & Hienenman, M. (1999). Comparing the wraparound process behavioral support: What we can learn. *Journal of Positive Behavior Interventions, 1*(3), 183–186.

McConaughy, S. H., Kay, P. J., & Fitzgerald, M. (1999). The achieving, behaving, caring project for preventing ED: Two-year outcomes. *Journal of Emotional and Behavioral Disorders, 7*(4), 224–239.

Purkey, W. W., Novak, J. M., & Schmidt, J. J. (1995). *Inviting school success: A self-concept approach to teaching, learning, and democratic practice.* Belmont, CA: Wadsworth.

Developing Positive Schoolwide Behavior Support Systems

Kartub, D. T., Taylor-Greene, S., March, R. E., & Horner, R. H. (2000). Reducing hallway noise: A systems approach. *Journal of Positive Behavior Interventions, 2*(3), 179–182.

Rockwell, S. (1993). *Tough to reach, tough to teach: Students with behavior problems.* Pacific Grove, CA: Brooks/Cole.

Todd, A. W., Horner, R. H., Sugai, G., & Sprague, J. R. (1999). Effective behavior support: Strengthening schoolwide systems through a team based approach. *Effective School Practices, 7*(4), 23–37.

Walker, H. M., Colvin, G., & Ramsey, E. (1995). *Antisocial behavior in school: Strategies and Best Practices.* Pacific Grove, CA: Brooks/Cole.

Implementing Contingency Management Systems

Response Cost Systems:

Gable, R. A., Arllen, N. L., & Rutherford, R. B. (1994). A note on the use of overcorrection. *Behavioral Disorders, 5*(3), 19–21.

Skiba, R. (1993). More than one way to get to the goal: The idea of behavioral covariation. *Beyond Behavior, 4*(3), 13–15.

Token Reinforcement Systems:

Barkley, R. A. (1996). 18 ways to make token systems more effective for ADHD children and teens. *The ADHD Report, 4*, 1–5.

Myles, B. S. (1992). Guidelines for establishing and maintaining token economies. *Intervention in School and Clinic, 27*(3), 164–169.

Structuring a Positive Environment

Dunlap, G., dePerczel, M., Clarke, S., Wilson, D., Wright, S., White, R., & Gomez, A. (1994). Choice making and proactive behavioral support for students with emotional and behavioral challenges. *Journal of Applied Behavioral Analysis, 27*, 505–518.

Kern, L., Mantegna, M. E., Vorndran, C. M., Bailin, D., & Hilt, A. (2001). Choice of task sequence to reduce problem behaviors. *Journal of Positive Behavior Intervention, 1*(2), 66–76, 122.

Ruef, M. B., Higgins, C., Glaeser, B. J. C., & Patnode, M. (1998). Positive behavioral support: Strategies for teachers. *Intervention, 34*(1), 21–32.

Using Positive Reinforcement

Mason, S. A., & Egel, A. L. (1995). What does Amy like? Using a mini-reinforcer assessment to increase student participation in instructional activities. *Teaching Exceptional Children, 28*(1), 42–45.

Northup, J., George, T., Jones, K., Broussard, C., & Vollmer, T. R. (1996). A comparison of reinforcer assessment methods: The utility of verbal and pictorial choice procedures. *Journal of Applied Behavior Analysis, 29*(2), 201–212.

Smith, M. (Ed.) (1993). *Behavior modification for exceptional children and youth.* Boston: Andover Medical.

Using Cognitive Behavioral Interventions

Brophy, J. (1996). *Teaching Problem Students.* New York: Guilford.

Hoff, K. E., & DuPaul, G. J. (1998). Reducing disruptive behavior in general education classrooms: The use of self-management strategies. *School Psychology Review, 27*(2), 290–303.

Marion, M. (1997). Guiding young children's understanding and management of anger. *Young Children, 52*(7), 62–67.

Special Series: Promoting Self-Determination (1995). *Intervention, 30*(3), 130–192.

Todd, A. W., Horner, R. H., & Sugai, G. (1999). Self-monitoring and self-recruited praise: Effects on problem behavior, academic engagement, and work completion in a typical classroom. *Journal of Positive Behavior Intervention, 1*(2), 66–76, 122.

Writing Behavior Modification Plans

Canter, L., & Canter, M. (1993). *Succeeding with difficult students.* Santa Monica, CA: Lee Canter and Associates.

Center for Effective Collaboration and Practice. (1998). *Addressing student problem behavior: An IEP team's introduction to functional behavioral assessment and behavior intervention plans.* Washington, DC: Author.

Dice, M. L. (1993). *Intervention strategies for children with emotional and behavioral disorders.* San Diego, CA: Singular.

Practical Ideas That Really Work
for Students with Disruptive, Defiant, or Difficult Behaviors

Preschool through Grade 4

Kathleen McConnell • Gail Ryser • James R. Patton

Evaluation Form

Behaviors addressed in this instrument are organized according to four categories. The relationship of these categories to the main themes of this resource are highlighted below.

Disruptive Behaviors
- Acting Out/Serious Misconduct

Defiant Behaviors
- Noncompliance in the Classroom

Difficult Behaviors
- Poor Peer Relationships
- Emotional Adjustment Problems

Student Name __Randi Meecham__

Birth Date __July 6, 1994__ Age __7__

School __Central Elementary__ Grade __2__

Educational Setting __general education__

Rater Name __Mr. Patrick Shaw__

Dates Student Observed: From __7-01__ To __1-02__

Amount of Time Spent with Student:

Per Day __6 hrs.__ Per Week __30 hrs.__

Behavior Problem(s) of Concern

1. __Constantly talks to friends during class time.__

2. __Does not follow classroom rules.__

3. __When reprimanded, Randi always has an excuse.__

Intervention(s) Previously Implemented

1. __Time out__

2. __Discussion with student__

3. __Call parents__

Figure 1. Sample Evaluation Form, filled out for Randi.

Rating Scale

DIRECTIONS

❶ In your opinion, to what degree are the listed behaviors a problem for the student? Use the following scale and circle the appropriate number:

0 = Never exhibits the behavior.
1 = Rarely exhibits the behavior so it is almost never a problem.
2 = Sometimes exhibits the behavior so at times it is a problem.
3 = Frequently exhibits the behavior so it often is a problem.
4 = Consistently exhibits the behavior so it almost always is a problem.

❷ Put a check in the appropriate box for items with a score of 3 or 4.

❸ On the Intervention Plan form on page 4, write in the behaviors with a score of 3 or 4; begin with those with a score of 4.

❹ For each behavior listed on the Intervention Plan form, select up to three intervention ideas from the Ideas Matrix on page 5 and fill in the idea numbers and start dates on the Intervention Plan form. Information relating to each intervention should be completed in the Notes column (e.g., effectiveness, adaptations made).

BEHAVIOR	RATING		SCORE OF 3 OR 4
	Never Rarely Sometimes Frequently Consistently		

Acting Out/Serious Misconduct (Disruptive Behaviors)

		Rating	3	4
1	Is verbally aggressive towards others.	(0) 1 2 3 4	☐	☐
2	Takes property from others without permission.	0 (1) 2 3 4	☐	☐
3	Leaves the classroom without permission.	(0) 1 2 3 4	☐	☐
4	Destroys or vandalizes property of others.	(0) 1 2 3 4	☐	☐
5	Fails to tell the truth.	0 (1) 2 3 4	☐	☐
6	Is physically aggressive towards others.	0 (1) 2 3 4	☐	☐
7	Uses profane or obscene language.	0 (1) 2 3 4	☐	☐
8	Avoids accepting responsibility for own behavior (e.g., blames others).	0 1 2 3 (4)	☐	☑
9	Is defiant toward authority.	0 1 (2) 3 4	☐	☐
10	Is unable to manage anger in an acceptable manner.	0 1 (2) 3 4	☐	☐

Noncompliance in the Classroom (Defiant Behaviors)

		Rating	3	4
1	Cheats on homework, quizzes, or tests.	(0) 1 2 3 4	☐	☐
2	Leaves seat without permission.	0 1 (2) 3 4	☐	☐
3	Is unable to work independently.	0 1 (2) 3 4	☐	☐
4	Has difficulty accepting constructive criticism.	0 1 (2) 3 4	☐	☐
5	Fails to complete assignments.	0 (1) 2 3 4	☐	☐
6	Contributes little or nothing when working on group activities.	0 1 (2) 3 4	☐	☐
7	Fails to follow classroom rules and procedures.	0 1 2 3 (4)	☐	☑
8	Fails to comply with teacher instructions (e.g., whines when asked to do something).	0 1 (2) 3 4	☐	☐
9	Is unprepared for class (e.g., does not bring materials, books, and supplies needed to class).	0 1 (2) 3 4	☐	☐
10	Disrupts teaching and learning by talking excessively, bothering others, and so on.	0 1 2 3 (4)	☐	☑

2

Figure 1. Continued.

BEHAVIOR	RATING	SCORE OF 3 OR 4

Poor Peer Relationships (Difficult Behaviors)

		Never	Rarely	Sometimes	Frequently	Consistently		
1	Bullies others.	(0)	1	2	3	4	☐	☐
2	Is avoided by peers.	0	1	(2)	3	4	☐	☐
3	Has difficulty expressing feelings of friendship.	0	(1)	2	3	4	☐	☐
4	Responds to teasing in inappropriate ways.	0	1	(2)	3	4	☐	☐
5	Avoids joining peers in playing games or in group activities.	0	(1)	2	3	4	☐	☐
6	Teases or taunts others.	(0)	1	2	3	4	☐	☐
7	Has difficulty laughing and joking with peers.	0	(1)	2	3	4	☐	☐
8	Has difficulty expressing empathy for peers.	0	1	(2)	3	4	☐	☐
9	Is rude to peers.	0	1	(2)	3	4	☐	☐
10	Rejects offers of friendship from peers.	0	(1)	2	3	4	☐	☐

Emotional Adjustment Problems (Difficult Behaviors)

		Never	Rarely	Sometimes	Frequently	Consistently		
1	Complains of aches, pains, or sickness.	0	1	(2)	3	4	☐	☐
2	Resists going to school.	0	1	(2)	3	4	☐	☐
3	Appears to be unhappy.	0	1	(2)	3	4	☐	☐
4	Appears to be anxious or fearful.	0	1	(2)	3	4	☐	☐
5	Talks pessimistically about the future.	(0)	1	2	3	4	☐	☐
6	Appears to be either excessively restless or excessively lethargic.	(0)	1	2	3	4	☐	☐
7	Shows little interest in most people or everyday events.	(0)	1	2	3	4	☐	☐
8	Has difficulty concentrating.	0	(1)	2	3	4	☐	☐
9	Has nervous habits (e.g., bites nails).	0	1	(2)	3	4	☐	☐
10	Avoids interactions with others.	0	(1)	2	3	4	☐	☐

Figure 1. Continued.

Intervention Plan

BEHAVIOR	INTERVENTION IDEA NUMBER	START DATE	NOTES
Disrupts teaching/learning	3	1-15-02	• very effective, positive
	22	1-15-02	• worked well, used stop in ASL
Avoids accepting responsibility	32		
	13		
Fails to follow classroom rules	3		
	7		• will use with entire class

4

Figure 1. Continued.

Ideas Matrix

	Ideas	Verbally Aggressive	Takes Property from Others	Leaves Classroom without Permission	Destroys Property of Others	Fails to Tell the Truth	Physically Aggressive	Uses Obscene Language	Doesn't Accept Responsibility	Defiant toward Authority	Unable to Manage Anger	Cheats	Leaves Seat	Unable to Work Independently	Difficulty Accepting Criticism	Fails to Complete Assignments	Doesn't Contribute to Activities	Doesn't Follow Classroom Rules	Doesn't Follow Instructions	Unprepared for Class	Disrupts Teaching and Learning
Acting Out/Serious Misconduct												**Noncompliance in the Classroom**									
1	Positive Post Cards	•	•	•	•	•	•	•	•	•	•	•	•	•	•	•	•	•	•	•	•
2	Little Things Mean a Lot	•	•	•	•	•	•	•	•	•	•	•	•	•	•	•	•	•	•	•	•
3	Ask Me About My Day	•	•	•	•	•	•	•	•	•	•	•	•	•	•	•	⊙	•	•	•	⊙
4	Good Relationships	•	•	•	•	•	•	•	•	•	•	•	•	•	•	•	•	•	•	•	•
5	In-School Mentors	•	•	•	•	•	•	•	•	•	•	•	•	•	•	•	•	•	•	•	•
6	Countdown	•										•	•	•	•	•	•	•	•	•	•
7	Turn It Around	•										•	•	•	•	•	⊙	•	•	•	•
8	Can Do & No Can Do	•	•	•	•	•	•	•	•	•											
9	Tic Tac Toe	•										•	•	•	•	•	•	•	•	•	•
10	Magic Money	•	•	•	•	•		•	•			•	•	•	•	•	•	•	•	•	•
11	Good News/Bad News	•	•	•	•	•	•	•	•			•	•	•	•	•	•	•	•	•	•
12	Our Hero	•	•	•	•	•	•	•	•	•		•	•	•	•	•	•	•	•	•	•
13	Follow the Leader			•					⊙				•	•	•	•	•	•	•	•	•
14	How Did I Do?	•	•				•	•	•	•		•	•	•	•	•	•	•	•	•	•
15	Track It	•	•	•	•	•	•	•	•	•	•	•	•	•	•	•	•	•	•	•	•
16	Talk Tickets																•	•	•	•	•
17	Just Say Yes								•	•			•	•	•		•	•	•		
18	It's How You Say It								•	•						•		•	•		•
19	Talk, Stop, & Walk	•						•	•	•			•	•				•	•		•
20	Nice/Not Nice	•									•										
21	I Spy Respect	•						•			•										
22	Hand Signs	•						•	•	•	•				•				•	•	⊙
23	Take a Break	•		•	•			•	•			•		•				•			•
24	Three Bs	•			•		•	•	•												
25	Copy the Rule	•		•	•			•	•					•							
26	Help Cards	•			•		•			•											
27	It Pays to Be Honest					•			•												
28	Stop, Think, & Choose	•	•	•	•	•	•	•	•	•		•						•	•		•
29	How It Feels		•		•							•	•	•	•	•	•	•	•	•	•
30	Positive Talk							•			•										
31	Games for the Group	•	•	•	•	•	•	•	•	•	•	•	•	•	•	•	•	•	•	•	•
32	Color On Cards	•	•	•	•	•	•	⊙	•	•		•	•	•	•	•	•	•	•	•	•
33	Here's Your Menu	•	•	•	•	•	•	•	•	•		•	•	•	•	•	•	•	•	•	•
34	Forms for You	•	•	•	•	•	•	•	•	•		•	•	•	•	•	•	•	•	•	•

Figure 1. Continued.

Ideas Matrix

Ideas	Bullies Others	Avoided By Peers	Difficulty Expressing Feelings	Inappropriate Response to Teasing	Avoids Peer Group Activities	Teases/Taunts Others	Difficulty Laughing/Joking	Difficulty Expressing Empathy	Rude to Peers	Rejects Offers of Empathy	Complains of Aches, Pains, Sickness	Resists Going to School	Appears Unhappy	Appears Anxious or Fearful	Talks Pessimistically	Excessively Restless or Lethargic	Little Interest in People or Events	Difficulty Concentrating	Nervous Habits	Avoids Interactions with Others
	Poor Peer Relationships										Emotional Adjustment Problems									
1 Positive Post Cards	•	•	•	•	•	•	•	•	•	•	•	•	•	•	•	•	•	•	•	•
2 Little Things Mean a Lot	•	•	•	•	•	•	•	•	•	•	•	•	•	•	•	•	•	•	•	•
3 Ask Me About My Day	•	•	•	•	•	•	•	•	•	•	•	•	•	•	•	•	•	•	•	•
4 Good Relationships	•	•	•	•	•	•	•	•	•		•		•	•						
5 In-School Mentors	•	•	•	•	•	•	•	•	•	•	•	•	•	•	•	•	•	•	•	•
6 Countdown																				
7 Turn It Around																				
8 Can Do & No Can Do	•					•		•											•	
9 Tic Tac Toe																				
10 Magic Money	•				•	•		•	•	•							•		•	
11 Good News/Bad News	•				•	•		•	•	•					•		•		•	
12 Our Hero	•	•	•		•	•	•	•			•			•	•		•	•	•	
13 Follow the Leader	•																			
14 How Did I Do?	•					•		•											•	
15 Track It	•	•	•	•	•	•	•	•	•	•	•	•	•	•	•	•	•	•	•	•
16 Talk Tickets					•													•		
17 Just Say Yes														•						
18 It's How You Say It																				
19 Talk, Stop, & Walk	•				•															
20 Nice/Not Nice	•	•	•			•	•		•				•							•
21 I Spy Respect	•	•	•	•	•	•	•	•	•								•			•
22 Hand Signs	•					•			•											
23 Take a Break	•								•											
24 Three Bs									•											
25 Copy the Rule	•					•			•											
26 Help Cards																				
27 It Pays to Be Honest																				
28 Stop, Think, & Choose	•					•		•												
29 How It Feels																				
30 Positive Talk	•	•				•		•	•		•		•	•	•	•	•	•	•	•
31 Games for the Group	•	•	•	•	•	•	•	•	•	•	•	•	•	•	•	•	•	•	•	•
32 Color On Cards	•	•	•	•	•	•	•	•	•	•	•	•	•	•	•	•	•	•	•	•
33 Here's Your Menu	•	•	•	•	•	•	•	•	•	•	•	•	•	•	•	•	•	•	•	•
34 Forms for You	•	•	•	•	•	•	•	•	•	•	•	•	•	•	•	•	•	•	•	•

6

Figure 1. Continued.

Idea 1
Positive Post Cards

Although all students love compliments and praise, lack of time may make it difficult for teachers to maintain positive communication with students and their families. One way to let parents know when their child does well is to mail positive notes directly to their homes. Use these templates to create easy-to-use post cards to reinforce students' positive accomplishments and good behavior. They will be most effective if used for specific behaviors like helping another student, making positive comments, sharing, or getting to class on time.

Directions: Copy on heavy stock paper, write a quick note, and mail.

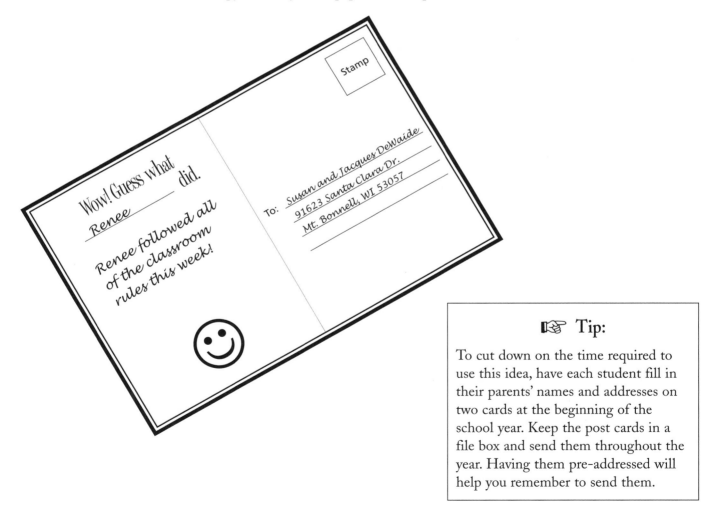

☞ **Tip:**

To cut down on the time required to use this idea, have each student fill in their parents' names and addresses on two cards at the beginning of the school year. Keep the post cards in a file box and send them throughout the year. Having them pre-addressed will help you remember to send them.

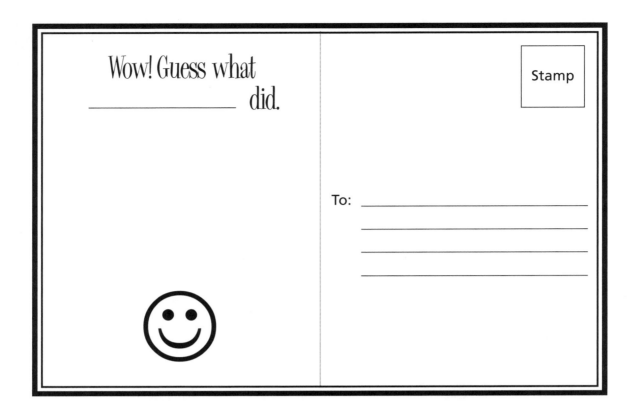

Wow! Guess what
_____ did.

Stamp

To: _____
_____
_____
_____

Wow! Guess what
_____ did.

Stamp

To: _____
_____
_____
_____

14

Idea 2
Little Things Mean a Lot

Teachers always appreciate quick and easy positive reinforcement methods that address several different behaviors. The format of Little Things Mean a Lot is a convenient method of praising all students and communicating with their families. The list format focuses student and teacher attention on a variety of high-quality, positive behaviors that contribute to positive peer relationships and school success. Encourage students to take these home to their parents. Use this one often!

Note. Idea provided by and used with permission of Joe Farley, 1998 Texas Teacher of the Year. (www.teamdiscipline.com)

Name _____   Date _____

Little Things Mean a Lot

 ♡ Helped a friend

 ♡ Tried hard

 ♡ Finished all your work

 ♡ Said something nice to someone

 ♡ Smiled

 ♡ Waited quietly

 ♡ Shared with a friend

 ♡ Listened to the teacher

Idea 2

Name _____ Date _____

Little Things Mean a Lot

❑ Came to school on time   ❑ Talked very softly

❑ Asked a good question   ❑ Tried hard

❑ Followed instructions   ❑ Tutored willingly

❑ Remembered a rule   ❑ Worked diligently

❑ Solved a problem   ❑ _____

Name _____ Date _____

Little Things Mean a Lot

❑ Apologized skillfully   ❑ Showed sportsmanship

❑ Accepted disappointment   ❑ Waited patiently

❑ Encouraged someone   ❑ Said something nice

❑ Reminded someone   ❑ Offered your help

❑ Requested nicely   ❑ _____

Idea 2

Idea 3
Go Ahead, Ask Me About My Day

Teachers are always looking for ways to get parents involved and "on their side" when it comes to students' behavior problems. It's not a good idea to wait until their child misbehaves to get in touch. Instead, make contact when a student has done well. Here is a great way to involve parents and make sure they know about their child's good behavior. It's very simple and easy to use:

When a student's behavior at school has been good, especially if it's been a long time between successes, present this coupon to the student and tell him or her to take it home and give it to a parent, grandparent, or other caregiver. After they ask about his or her day, the student can do a little bragging, get some well deserved praise and pats on the back, and know you have set him or her up for this positive experience. It's a win/win/win situation!

 Go ahead, ask me about my day at school.

 Go ahead, ask me about my day at school.

 Go ahead, ask me about my day at school.

 Go ahead, ask me about my day at school.

 Go ahead, ask me about my day at school.

 Go ahead, ask me about my day at school.

 Go ahead, ask me about my day at school.

 Go ahead, ask me about my day at school.

Idea 3

Idea 4
There's No Substitute for a Good Relationship

All students like to know that people care about them. All teachers have long recognized the importance of establishing and maintaining positive relationships with students. These relationships can affect many facets of education, including students' motivation and their responses to praise or punishment. Unfortunately, it can sometimes be difficult to build close relationships with students who are withdrawn, challenging, or in need of lots of support. Here are some simple forms to help you keep track of information about your students. By themselves, they cannot ensure good, positive relationships. However, they do provide a format to begin to communicate—always the first step in any good relationship!

There are two forms for your use. The first is an information/interview form. Use the form as a way to begin to get to know each student. The interview may take at least 5 to 10 minutes per student, which adds up to a lot of time; however, it may be the most important time you spend in preventing behavior problems, connecting with students who feel alone, or just getting to know students whom you may otherwise never notice. The second form is a simple birthday calendar you can use to list students' birthdays throughout the year. This will help you make each student's birthday a little special and also let him or her know you care, even if all you do is give a verbal congratulations. Make sure to include all students by having a "Summer Birthday Celebration."

Student Information and Interview Form

Student's Name Lakita Sherman
Nickname Kita
Birthday June 6
Parents'/Guardians' Names and Telephone Numbers   Work 456-3660
Mother Joyce Sherman   Work 456-6897
   Home 456-8213
Father Marcus Sherman
   Home 456-8213

Interview Questions

1. Who are your best friends here at school?
   Shirley Jackson and Marilyn Smith
2. What are your favorite subjects/activities in school?
   story time, centers, math
3. What are your favorite activities/hobbies out of school?
   dancing, singing, swimming
4. What is one thing you are good at?
   playing kick ball
5. What kind of help do you need most from your teachers?
   I need help with reading. It's hard.
6. What is one thing you would like me to know about you?
   I am the fastest runner in my class.
7. How do you get home from school?
   My dad picks me up.

Student Information and Interview Form

Student's Name _____
Nickname _____
Birthday _____

Parents'/Guardians' Names and Telephone Numbers
    Mother _____
              Home _____   Work _____
    Father _____
              Home _____   Work _____

Interview Questions

1. Who are your best friends here at school?

_____

2. What are your favorite subjects/activities in school?

_____

3. What are your favorite activities/hobbies out of school?

_____

4. What is one thing you are good at?

_____

5. What kind of help do you need most from your teachers?

_____

6. What is one thing you would like me to know about you?

_____

7. _____

_____

Idea 4

Birthday Calendar

Name	January	February	March	April	May	June	July	August	September	October	November	December

Idea 4

Idea 5
In-School Mentors

Students who are alienated or who have difficulty making and keeping friendships often feel very alone at school. These students may also have behavioral problems when they try to get attention or join in group activities but don't know how. Their attempts to socialize or "fit in" may actually cause peers or adults to stay away from them.

One easy way for teachers to help a student build at least one positive relationship is to become an informal mentor. While teachers may not have time in the school day to tutor, read, or help a student study, they often have enough time to let the student know they care. We have provided some ready-made notes so that communication can be quick and easy.

Here are some ways to encourage a student.

❶ Give the student a friendly note on his or her birthday or other holiday.

❷ Have lunch together once every 2 weeks.

❸ Meet the student before or after school for 10 minutes once a week.

❹ Call the student at home when he or she has done a great job on something at school.

❺ Surprise the student with a special pen, book, or notebook.

❻ Offer to help the student study during lunch period every other Wednesday.

❼ Lend an ear and a hand when he or she has a problem or gets in trouble.

☞ Tip:

You may want to vary this idea by becoming a "Secret Friend" to a student. With this approach, no one knows who his or her special friend is until the relationship has been established. Then everyone in the school who is involved in the program gets together for a surprise breakfast and each student tries to guess which teacher has been his or her secret friend.

You Are Special

26

Happy Birthday!

Way To Go!

_____

_____

_____

_____

_____

_____

28

Idea 5

Idea 6
Countdown to Good Behavior

Here's a group management strategy that works for all students, regardless of age. It includes a systematic way of warning students that encourages consistency and doesn't provide teacher attention for misbehavior.

Here's how it works.

❶ Create a sign that is large enough for all students in the class to see. The sign should have the numbers 5-4-3-2-1 in vertical order. If possible, use bright, appealing colors and make sure the sign is large enough for all students to see from anywhere in the classroom. We have provided a form that you can enlarge for class use or use as is for individual students.

❷ Attach a large clip or arrow on the side of the sign by the number 5. This will be your starting point while teaching.

❸ Decide on your target behaviors. Start with the basics necessary for direct instruction:
- Stay seated
- Raise your hand before talking.

❹ Explain to your students that if they have to be warned four or fewer times during the lesson, the whole class will have a special activity. You can create a menu of ideas that your students really like, including:
- Extra recess time
- Five minutes to talk to friends at the end of class
- Read aloud time
- Extra drinks at the water fountain
- Popcorn party on Friday

☞ **Tip:**

Use 5-4-3-2-1 the first semester and 3-2-1 after students have had time to learn the system and practice following the rules.

Note. This idea is adapted from *Project Ride: Responding to Individual Differences in Education, Elementary School Edition,* by R. Beck, 1996, Longmont, CO: Sopris West. Copyright 1996 by Sopris West. Adapted with permission.

❺ Begin your direct instruction lesson. Keep it short the first few times (5 to 10 minutes.) If students fail to follow either of the two rules, move the clip down from the 5 to the 4. Look directly at the student who has talked out or been out of his or her seat but do not stop teaching to reprimand him or her or otherwise provide attention.

❻ Finally, at the end of the lesson, compliment students if they still have a number and provide the selected reinforcer. If there have been too many warnings, try again.

Idea 7
Turn It Around

One fun way to encourage good behavior from an entire class is to play a game called "Turn It Around." Before the week, day, or class period begins, select a group privilege, activity, or other reward that the whole class will enjoy. Limit your selection to a word or short phrase, then write each letter of the reward on a separate 8½ × 11 card. Since the number of letters in the reward will determine how long it takes for students to earn their privilege, choose a short word for younger students and a longer word or phrase for older students. Here are some examples that most students will like:

CANDY FOR ALL

ICE CREAM SUNDAES

FRIDAY CUPCAKES

MORE RECESS

MUSIC

TALK 5 MINUTES

PLAY A GAME WITH A FRIEND

WIGGLE TIME

| P | I | Z | Z | A | | P | A | R | T | Y |

Here's how it works.

❶ Post the letters at the front of the classroom so they are visible to everyone. Make sure they are facing the wall or board. You can tack them to a tacking strip; attach them to a bulletin board with Velcro, or use clothespins and a line to secure them across the front of the room.

Note. Idea provided by and used with permission of Alisa Kulak, Pine Tree Elementary School, Longview, Texas.

❷ The next step is to identify a specific behavior that students should demonstrate and specify a time period that you will evaluate it. For example,

• No talking out for 5 minutes
• Stay seated for the whole lesson
• Everyone answers once
• Everyone tries his or her best
• Everyone brings a pencil today
• Stay in line in the hall.

❸ If the students meet the criterion, then they get to turn a letter around. The next time they do well, another letter gets turned, until all have been revealed and the students have earned their special reward.

☞ Tip 1:

To make things more exciting, you might want to choose individual students to turn around letters in random order. This will keep them guessing about what they'll be earning.

☞ Tip 2:

If your students cannot read, use a picture puzzle format. Cut a large photo or drawing into pieces and assemble the puzzle. We have provided a pizza puzzle for you to use as a start.

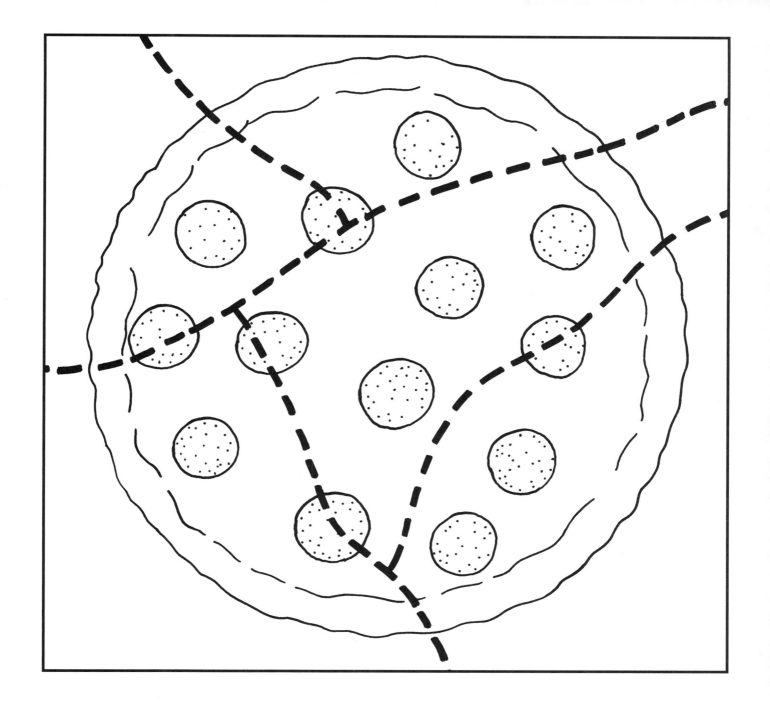

Idea 8
Can Do and No Can Do

Even though we would like to improve students' behavior by using only positive reinforcement, sometimes that is not possible. It may be necessary and helpful to use some mild punishment as a consequence of misbehavior. Here is an idea that is a version of a technique often called *cost response*. The principle involved in any cost response strategy is that students start out with or earn some privileges or goodies but lose them if they misbehave. This approach works best if specific behaviors are targeted, so that students and teachers can focus on improving important, highly valued skills. This strategy can be used with individual students, with a group, or with an entire class.

Here's how Can Do and No Can Do works.

❶ First, locate some basic materials. You will need:
- Two small cans, such as one-pound coffee cans or small icing cans. You will probably want to have lids for the cans, especially if you want to maintain some secrecy and suspense.
- Two labels—one that says "Can Do" and one that says "No Can Do."
- Small coupons, tongue depressors, craft sticks, or tiny strips of paper like those found in fortune cookies.
- A menu of privileges and rewards from which students can select their favorites. You can use the menu provided in Idea 33, Here's Your Menu, or create your own.

❷ Next, talk with your class or student. Select five of the positive reinforcers that he or she (or they) prefer and would like to earn. If you are using this idea with a class, they can vote or you can let individual students select their favorite rewards on a rotating schedule. Students should also be encouraged to contribute new ideas, so that the reinforcers change each day or week.

❸ Write the list of the five favorite reinforcers on the board so that everyone can see what they are trying to earn. Also write each reinforcer on a slip of paper, or use a marker to write each reinforcer on a tongue depressor or craft stick. If students cannot read, replace words with simple line drawings.

We have provided some examples of reinforcers in a coupon format that you can use, but feel free to get creative and design your own.

❹ Decide on a schedule for drawing a reinforcer from the can. This can be once or twice a day, once per week, etc. However, make sure you don't wait too long or students will lose interest.

❺ Explain clearly to students how the Can Do and No Can Do process will work. At the beginning of the day, period, or week, the five selected privileges (in the form of a stick, coupon, or slip of paper) are placed into the Can Do can. Students are reminded of the target behavior. As long as everyone follows the rule or demonstrates the key behavior, all of the privileges remain in the Can Do can. However, if someone breaks the rule or engages in a disruptive or negative behavior, one privilege is removed and placed in the No Can Do can. This means that the privilege is no longer available. When removing a privilege or goodie, you can either tell students which opportunity they have lost, or you can keep it a secret, so that the reinforcers still available are a mystery. Each time students misbehave, one positive reinforcer is moved from the Can Do to the No Can Do can.

❻ At the end of the class period, day, or week, select a student to close his or her eyes and draw the reinforcer from among those left in the Can Do can. Before drawing the reinforcer, hype it up, get excited, and build some suspense. If you work with sticks, rattle the can and make the drawing exciting.

❼ After the positive reinforcement has been selected and provided, celebrate and have fun. If students missed out on the best reinforcers because of misbehavior, review the rules or target behavior and encourage them to try to do better next time.

❽ Repeat the process but change reinforcers often. Use the most powerful reinforcers you have for difficult or stressful times (right before spring break, Fridays, after a long weekend, etc.).

39

Can Do Coupon
This coupon entitles you to a **special pen or pencil**.

Can Do Coupon
This coupon entitles the group to **special pencils**.

Can Do Coupon
This coupon entitles you to a **fancy folder or book cover**.

Can Do Coupon
This coupon entitles the group to **extra recess**.

Can Do Coupon
This coupon entitles you to **special stickers**.

Can Do Coupon
This coupon entitles the group to **candy and fruit drinks**.

Can Do Coupon
This coupon entitles you to **call your parents and tell them what a good job you did**.

Can Do Coupon
This coupon entitles the group to a **sundae party**.

Can Do Coupon
This coupon entitles you to **visit the principal for recognition**.

Can Do Coupon
This coupon entitles the group to **listen to music**.

Can Do Coupon
This coupon entitles you to

_____

Can Do Coupon
This coupon entitles the group to

_____

Idea 9
Behavior Tic Tac Toe

Here's a fun game that all students enjoy. It involves playing a game of Tic Tac Toe focused on 100% behavior. Every student in the class should demonstrate 100% behaviors because they have a significant effect on instruction, classroom management, or students' relationships with others. All you have to do is select a behavior, challenge your students, and let the game begin. If students win, they get an agreed upon privilege for the whole class.

Here's what to do to get ready.

❶ Create a large tic, tac, toe square and post it at the front of the room. You could also use the sample provided here on an overhead projector, or draw a square on the board.

❷ Pick a symbol for each side (X for the teacher and O for the students or vice versa).

❸ Ask students what they would like to earn. Go for privileges and responsibilities first since these are usually important to students and won't cost money.

❹ Select the behavior you would like to improve. Some of the behaviors that would work for this game include:
  • Following a direction within 20 seconds. ("I'm starting my stopwatch. If everyone follows my direction within 20 seconds, you can make a play on the Tic Tac Toe board. If I see someone failing to respond, I get a move.")
  • Smile and say, "hi." ("When you enter the classroom, I'll be standing by the door. I will say 'Hi' and smile at you. Please do the same. You get to put up an X if everyone does this; if not, I get an O.")
  • No put-downs. ("We treat each other with respect. If I don't hear any put-downs for the next half hour, you get a turn at tic tac toe. If anyone puts someone else down, I get a turn.")

41

❺ If all students meet the behavior goal, they get to put up an X or O; if not, the teacher gets a turn. If students win the game, everyone in the class earns the reinforcer. If the teacher wins, students "owe" him or her something. For example, students might all give the teacher a hug as they leave the class.

❻ Repeat often enough so that students stay focused on the behavior and don't lose interest. Play several times each morning or afternoon, and repeat each day until someone wins.

☞ Tip:

Suggestions for group reinforcers can be found in Idea 8, Can Do and No Can Do, and in Idea 33, Here's Your Menu.

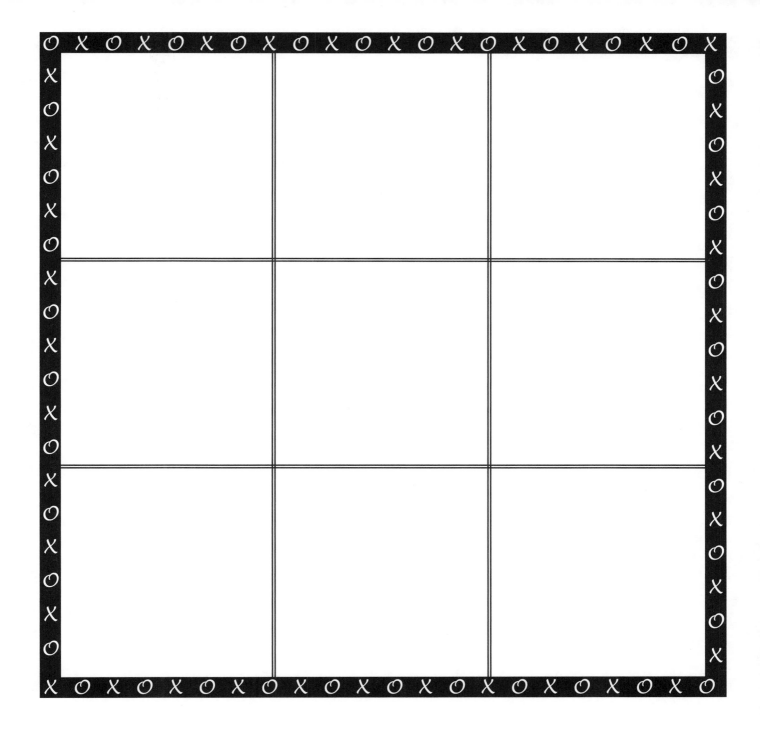

Idea 9

Idea 10
Magic Money

Often, the more clear and thorough a behavior management system is the easier it is for teachers to implement. While systems make take some time to design, construct, and establish, the payoff can be well worth the effort if it works. Systems that include ways to earn and spend money, as well as fines, savings accounts, and bonuses are used by many teachers to encourage positive behaviors and discourage misbehavior. Magic Money is a simple way to establish a classroom management system. (Icons provided in Appendix B.)

Here's how the system works.

❶ Identify the most important behaviors, prioritizing from the least critical (e.g., staying in seat) to behaviors that are absolutely not permitted (e.g., hitting others).

❷ Discuss with the students what amounts will be earned for positive behaviors and what fines will be charged for problem behaviors. Represent each behavior with a picture or symbol.

❸ Let the students help create a list of rewards and a value for each.

❹ Decide on a spending schedule. Select small items for the day (e.g., soda at lunch) and big ones (e.g., computer time) for the end of the week and the month.

❺ Make sure everyone is clear about the system and how they will be evaluated. *Be consistent*.

☞ **Tip:**

Use a notebook to keep track of the students' accounts. Keep the Magic Money in a lockable bag or box, and store it at school.

Magic Money

Earn Magic Money by:

$_____$ $_____$

You will lose Magic Money if you:

$_____$ $_____$

You can buy these rewards with Magic Money

$_____$ $_____$

Idea 10

Idea 11
Good News/Bad News

To communicate clearly with students about the positive and negative consequences of their actions, it is helpful to use a visual organization tool like the Good News/Bad News chart. This chart spells out exactly what will happen if students follow the rules and what will happen if they do not.

Using the Good News/Bad News chart should help you remain consistent in your responses. In addition, argumentative students can be dealt with by pointing to the chart instead of discussing circumstances and options. This should help students learn that they are responsible for making choices about their behavior and that their choices will determine what happens next. (Icons provided in Appendix B.)

Here's how to use the chart.

❶ In the first few days of school, discuss with students what they think should be the consequences for following and not following the class rules.

❷ List their ideas, along with your own, on the chart. As you list the consequences, start with the least intensive and intrusive consequences. Gradually increase the intensity, frequency, and severity (or appeal) as you complete the list.

❸ Give each student a copy of the Good News/Bad News form and post an enlarged copy in your class.

❹ When students follow the rules, be sure you call attention to their behavior and reward them with a Good News intervention. If they fail to follow the class rules, use your continuum of interventions to apply negative or punishing consequences.

Note. The chart is based on an idea in *The Tough Kid Tool Box* by W. R. Jenson, G. Rhode, and H. K. Reavis, 1994–1995, Longmont, CO: Sopris West. Copyright 1994–1995 by Sopris West.

There's Some Good News and There's Some Bad News

about Following Class Rules

The Good News Is	The Bad News Is
1.	1.
2.	2.
3.	3.
4.	4.
5.	5.

Idea 11

There's Some
Good News

and

(about following class rules)

There's Some
Bad News

☺   ☹

1.

2.

3.

1.

2.

3.

Idea 11

Idea 12
Our Hero

In most educational settings today, classes include a diverse group of students who demonstrate a wide range of behaviors. Some students generally follow the rules, participate actively, and cause few problems while others seem to consistently experience difficulties and challenge their teachers' patience and endurance. Nevertheless, most teachers refuse to give up and are always looking for strategies to improve the behavior of all students. Our Hero is an idea specifically designed to encourage each student to do his or her best, regardless of prior behaviors and attitudes.

To use Our Hero, follow these steps.

❶ Target one specific behavior for improvement. Explain to students what the behavior is, provide examples and nonexamples, and tell them how you will evaluate performance of this behavior. Some useful behaviors to target include:

- Finishes the class work assignment
- Takes turns
- Compliments or makes a positive comment to another student
- Answers at least one question in class
- Says "Yes, ma'am" or "Yes, sir" when given a direction
- Gets to class on time
- Smiles at least one time during the class period

❷ Also discuss with students a group privilege or reward that they would like to earn and you feel comfortable providing. You will find a Class Privilege Menu in Idea 33 that suggests some rewards that students usually like.

❸ Have each student write his or her name on the hero card. Mix the cards up and put them face down in a stack. You can put them in a small basket or wrap them in a rubber band to keep them organized.

Our Hero

Our target behavior is: _Keeping our hands_
to ourselves

We will earn a privilege if our hero demonstrates the target behavior by: _Not hitting, pushing, or_
bothering other students in the class

❹ Each day, draw a card from the stack and *without looking at the name* put it in a brightly colored, large (9 x 11) envelope that is labeled, "Our Hero." Seal the envelope and tape or tack it to the board or wall at the front of the room.

❺ At the end of the specified period of time—the morning, afternoon, class period, or day—open the envelope. Look at the name and then decide if the student has demonstrated the target behavior, according to your prior criteria.

❻ After a short drum roll (or other "build up"), repeat the target behavior, and say, "Today's hero is _____, who has earned a privilege for the whole class because he or she has demonstrated the target behavior of _____."

❼ If the student has not met the criteria for being the hero, simply say, "We have no hero today because this student did not demonstrate the target behavior." Do not tell students the name of this student, just return to card to the stack to try again the next time.

Our Hero

Our target behavior is: _____

_____

_____

We will earn a privilege if our hero demonstrates
the target behavior by:_____

_____

_____

_____

Our Hero Is Inside

Our Hero Is
_____

Our Hero Is
_____

Our Hero Is
_____

Our Hero Is
_____

Our Hero Is
_____

Our Hero Is
_____

Our Hero Is
_____

Our Hero Is
_____

Idea 12

Idea 13
Follow the Leader

Here's a great way to target students' performance on a key classroom skill: following directions. Following directions is a critical skill because it often prevents other related misbehaviors from occurring and when students comply quickly, an effective pace of instruction can be maintained. The Follow the Leader strategy is useful because it combines an intervention technique with a method of data collection so that daily progress can be easily reviewed. While most teachers recognize that it's a good idea to keep track of progress, the actual collection and review of data can be a daunting task. Fortunately, recording, tracking and evaluating behavioral data doesn't have to be difficult or time consuming, as you'll see if you use Follow the Leader in your classroom. Follow the Leader can be used with all students, either individually or as a group management technique.

Here is how to implement this idea.

❶ First, copy the Follow the Leader chart. Make a large poster-sized copy if you are working with a group or a small copy if you are targeting just one student.

❷ Each time you give a direction, circle a number on the chart.

❸ Give the student(s) 10 to 20 seconds to comply with your request. If you are working with a large group, scan the group to see if everyone has followed your direction.

❹ If the student(s) has followed the direction, compliment him or her and put a slash mark over the circled number. If not, leave the number with a circle and move on to the next task or request without providing the student(s) a lot of attention for the misbehavior.

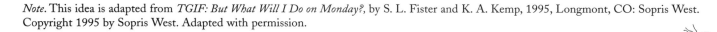

Note. This idea is adapted from *TGIF: But What Will I Do on Monday?*, by S. L. Fister and K. A. Kemp, 1995, Longmont, CO: Sopris West. Copyright 1995 by Sopris West. Adapted with permission.

❺ At the end of the instructional or class period, look over the chart to determine the number of times direction was followed. If students are not following your directions at least 8 out of 10 times, you may want to target this skill for improvement.

❻ One way to improve direction following is to set a goal for improvement. For example, if students have been following directions only 6 out of 10 times, try to improve performance to 7, then 8, and eventually 9 out of 10 times. You can use several strategies to improve the direction-following percentage:
- Talk to the student and set a goal, a date of desired mastery, and a reward if the goal is reached.
- Have students evaluate their own performance each day by asking themselves how they did. Use the graph to evaluate progress.
- Work with your administrator to establish a system of rewards and consequences for following directions. For example, students who reach the 9 out of 10 goal will get to have a special lunch with the principal; students below 5 out of 10 will have a conference with the principal and their parents.

☞ Tip:

Follow the Leader is a very useful strategy to include in Behavioral Intervention Plans (BIPs) for students with disabilities. The built-in data collection system provides a way to set a specific goal and then monitor progress.

Follow the Leader

 1 2 3 4 5 6 7 8 9 10 ___ of 10

 1 2 3 4 5 6 7 8 9 10 ___ of 10

 1 2 3 4 5 6 7 8 9 10 ___ of 10

 1 2 3 4 5 6 7 8 9 10 ___ of 10

 1 2 3 4 5 6 7 8 9 10 ___ of 10

Idea 13

Follow the Leader

How am I doing?

10
9
8
7
6
5
4
3
2
1
0

DATE

Idea 13

Idea 14
How Did I Do?

One simple way to teach students to monitor and control their own behavior is to encourage self-evaluation. It may be necessary to first model for students some self-talk, then give them a simple tool to evaluate themselves on specific behaviors. (Icons provided in Appendix B.)

Here is one self-evaluation strategy.

❶ First, describe a specific behavior that you would like to see or hear students doing in class. If possible, use an action verb to describe the behavior. For example, you might specify one of these common expectations for behavior:
  • Listen while the teacher talks
  • Stay at your center until you hear the signal
  • Raise your hand for help

❷ Next, teach students to occasionally check up on their own behavior. You can do this by modeling some self-talk. Use phrases such as,
  • Am I listening?
  • Am I in my center?
  • Did I raise my hand for help?
  Say the phrase for students, then have them repeat it. Do this again about halfway through the activity to be sure students are staying focused on their behavior.

❸ Next, give students an opportunity to practice asking themselves the question out loud as a group. ("Am I listening?")

❹ Then, proceed with the lesson or activity.

❺ When students have completed the assignment, suggest that they now ask themselves, "How did I do?" on the specific behavior. After they silently ask the question, they can fill out the simple rating form.

❻ Use the rating forms as the basis for discussion and feedback with the entire class or individual students. Help students improve their self-evaluation and teach them to set goals for improvement.

☞ Tip:

Specify individual behaviors by filling in the blank with a picture (we have provided some examples) or phrase that describes the desired behavior.

How Did I Do?

How did I do with _____?

Circle a face to show how you did.

☺ 😐 ☹

To do better next time, I will _____.

Name _____ Date_____

How Did I Do?

How did I do on _____?

(Circle a number.)

1	2	3
Great	Okay	Not very well

What should I do differently next time?

_____

_____

Name _____ Date_____

How Did I Do?

How did I do on _____?

(Circle a number.)

1	2	3
Great	Okay	Not very well

What should I do differently next time?

_____

_____

Idea 15
Track It

Students often learn from monitoring and tracking their own performance, two skills that may lead to better self-management. Here is a quick and easy way that students can track their own behavior and evaluate their progress, whether it in increasing desirable, positive behaviors or decreasing negative or disruptive behaviors.

The tracking form provided is easy to use; all the student has to do is color in or put a mark in a box each time the behavior occurs. The chart can be used for several minutes or for full days, but the same amount of time should be used for each tracking session. When the chart is completed, count the number of marked boxes and write the total in the circle at the top. A ready-made progress graph can be created by drawing a line to connect the top marked boxes on a page.

Students can learn to chart any behavior that can be counted.

- Talking out (or raising hand before talking)
- Staying seated
- Keeping hands to self
  - Keeping quiet during quiet time
  - Following class rules
  - Saying "Yes" or "Okay"
  - Making positive (or negative) comments
  - Asking for help
  - Offering to help others
- Asking a question

☞ Tip:

The charts can be used as part of a contract. Simply monitor students before intervening, then set a target goal and let them begin to record their progress.

Track It

										TOTAL
10	9	8	7	6	5	4	3	2	1	

DATE _____

TIME INTERVAL _____

										TOTAL
10	9	8	7	6	5	4	3	2	1	

DATE _____

TIME INTERVAL _____

										TOTAL
10	9	8	7	6	5	4	3	2	1	

DATE _____

TIME INTERVAL _____

										TOTAL
10	9	8	7	6	5	4	3	2	1	

DATE _____

TIME INTERVAL _____

										TOTAL
10	9	8	7	6	5	4	3	2	1	

DATE _____

TIME INTERVAL _____

Idea 15

Idea 16
Talk Tickets

All students can benefit from these questioning techniques.

❶ Begin the question with a student's name.
"Gail, what is 2 + 2?"
➤ This focuses the student's attention *before* you ask the question and keeps him or her "with you."

❷ Have students question a partner after you model the type of question.
"Turn to your partner and ask him or her what word begins with the letter B?"
➤ This allows students to get information from each other and teaches them what to ask themselves during a lesson.

❸ Alternate individual and group questions.
"Everyone who thinks the answer is 5, hold up your hand. Now, Leroy, tell me what you did first."
➤ Group responses are quick and don't interupt the flow of the lesson. They are also an effective and efficient method of assessing how much the class is learning from your instruction. For a more complete assessment, combine group responses with individual questioning, which is critical for measuring individual students' progress.

❹ Ask both open-ended and specific recall types of questions.
"What kind of house do we find in our neighborhoods?" "Why do you think so?"
➤ Students are often great at getting the big idea but may miss the details. They not only need a chance to shine with open-ended questions but also to practice focusing with more specific questions.

❺ Use a ticket (provided on the next page) or token system to make sure everyone takes a turn answering your questions and no one monopolizes the conversation.
Pass out one ticket to each student. Have the students hand you their tickets as they answer a question. Once a student has answered and handed in the ticket, it is someone else's turn.
➤ This strategy encourages talkative students to limit their talk-outs and may help reluctant students to become more actively involved.

Note. This idea is from *Practical Ideas That Really Work for Students with ADHD*, by K. McConnell, G. Ryser, and J. Higgins, 1999, Austin, TX: PRO-ED, Inc. Copyright 1999 by PRO-ED, Inc. Reprinted with permission.

Talk Ticket
The bearer of this ticket
is permitted to talk
1 Time

Talk Ticket
The bearer of this ticket
is permitted to talk
1 Time

Talk Ticket
The bearer of this ticket
is permitted to talk
1 Time

Talk Ticket
The bearer of this ticket
is permitted to talk
1 Time

Talk Ticket
The bearer of this ticket
is permitted to talk
1 Time

Talk Ticket
The bearer of this ticket
is permitted to talk
1 Time

Talk Ticket
The bearer of this ticket
is permitted to talk
1 Time

Talk Ticket
The bearer of this ticket
is permitted to talk
1 Time

Talk Ticket
The bearer of this ticket
is permitted to talk
1 Time

Talk Ticket
The bearer of this ticket
is permitted to talk
1 Time

Talk Ticket
The bearer of this ticket
is permitted to talk
1 Time

Idea 16

Idea 17
Just Say Yes

Students have many ways of refusing to follow directions or comply with requests. Some students sit passively and ignore the adult talking to them. Others put their heads down and fall asleep. Many students actively refuse to do what adults ask and argue, complain, ask unrelated questions, or say, "No."

One way to encourage a positive verbal response is to ask the student to make an affirmative verbal response and then follow the direction. Saying "yes" (or a version of yes) is often a first step in a more cooperative pattern of behavior. Eventually, we hope each student will not only verbalize a positive response to a request or direction but also complete the requested action. For teachers, hearing "yes" is music to their ears and often indicates that a student may be ready to improve their direction-following behavior.

Here are three quick ways to get a yes.

❶ **Give students reminders and a structured method of encouragement.** For young students, use a desktop contract that focuses on a pattern of positive responses. This kind of visual system allows students to monitor their own progress and then receive reinforcement after consistent improvement. Tape the contract to a corner of the student's desk so that it also serves as a reminder to follow directions. The contract can be in a puzzle format like our example or any other you choose.

❷ Teach students some nonverbal cues and use them to get students moving after a direction. Here are some examples of nonverbal reminders and ways to say "yes":

- *Teacher* walks by a student's desk and points to an assignment or task. *Student* nods head and begins.

- *Teacher* holds up three fingers and counts them down silently as a signal to be quiet and begin.
  Student gives a "thumbs up" sign.
- *Teacher* makes eye contact with students who have not yet followed directions.
  Student responds by signing "yes" in American Sign Language. This is an easy sign to teach—closed fist with fist making a head-nodding motion. (See illustration.)

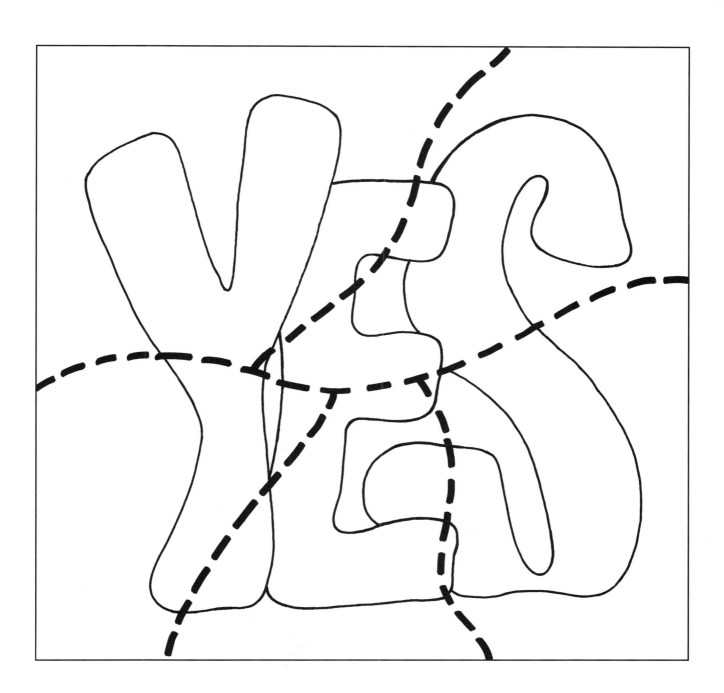

Idea 17

Directions: Write down a parent's work or home telephone number. Each time the student says "yes" and follows a direction, the student highlights an appropriate number button. When the predetermined number of telephone buttons are highlighted, he or she gets to make a positive phone call to Mom or Dad and the teacher brags about their progress. (This must be approved by parents ahead of time). If someone at school has a cell phone with free long distance, the students could call a grandparent, aunt or uncle, or friend anywhere in the United States.

Their Phone Number is _____

Idea 18
It's Not What You Say, It's How You Say It

When dealing with students, sometimes the way you communicate is just as important as the message you are sending. In particular, students who are oppositional-defiant or just plain stubborn often have difficulties responding to teacher requests or accepting "no" for an answer. Here are some quick tips for gaining cooperation without arguing with students.

Here are a few examples.

❶ **Use the phrase, "Yes, if . . ."** When students make frequent requests to do or get things, you don't always have to say no. Sometimes the phrase, "Yes, if . . . ." will accomplish the same thing as the word "no" but without setting up an argument. This also allows you to be clear about your expectations.

❷ **Follow Grandma's Rule: "First, do this; then you can do that."** This rule has been around for years but it is still very effective when used with many students. When students beg, whine, wheedle, and protest to get their own way, they may escalate teachers' reactions. However, if you plan ahead, stay calm, and use this phrase, you can often encourage cooperation and compliance without a fight.

❸ **Fall back on the "Broken Record" technique.** When students are argumentative and reluctant to give up their opinions or desires, sometimes the best approach is just to keep on repeating your own request. Don't explain, argue, discuss, or accept excuses. Just repeat your request.

❹ **Build momentum by asking the "easy stuff" first.** One way to get oppositional students to cooperate and comply with requests is to build a sequence or chain of positive behaviors. You can do this by making simple requests first. Ask the student to do things he or she ordinarily would do anyway (e.g., have a seat, relax, get out your book). Then at the end of the sequence, add the more challenging request (e.g., Please answer the first question.).

❺ **Use the phrase, "Instead of _____, do _____."** To redirect students, tell them what to do instead of what they are doing.

☞ **Tip:**
These ideas are also useful for parents, so don't hesitate to share them with your students' families.

Idea 19
Talk, Stop, and Walk

This is a wonderful communication technique to use with students who are constantly trying to wheedle, whine, or argue; anything to avoid following directions. This idea is based on a strategy called "Speak 'n Spin" by Linda Classen, an educator in Texas.

Here's how Talk, Stop, and Walk works.

❶ Talk

When a student is misbehaving, look the student in the eye and calmly describe the behavior in two or three words. For example, "That's arguing." Or "That's talking out."

❷ Stop

At the same time, make the stop sign with your arm by putting your hand out with the palm facing the student. This is the visual cue to "stop."

❸ Talk

Next, use two or three words to request the behavior you want to see. For example, "Show me waiting." Or "Show me listening."

❹ Walk

Then, break eye contact and turn or walk away from the student. If the student follows your direction, reinforce him or her immediately.

❺ Talk

If the student does not comply with your request, then talk again, this time explaining the contingency or deal that is in place.
- If you do what is asked, then you can get what you want. If I have to ask again, you will lose a privilege or reinforcer. (For example, "If you listen, then you can have your whole recess time, but if I have to ask you again, then you will lose the first 5 minutes of recess.")

❻ Walk

Then no more talking.

☞ **Tip:**

This is a good technique to rehearse and practice, so that you follow all the steps. Remember, the more consistent you are, the more effective this strategy will be. This is also a great idea to share with parents.

Idea 20
Nice/Not Nice

All students will get along better with peers if they make positive rather than negative statements or comments. Saying nice things can increase students' expressions of empathy and shared experiences, reduce teasing or rudeness, and help students develop friendships.

The Nice/Not Nice form will help you work with students to set goals for positive talk. It can later be used as a student self-monitoring form or a contract. (Icons provided in Appendix B.)

Here's how it works.

❶ First, demonstrate for students some examples of positive comments (nice talk). These can include compliments, offers to help, praise for a job well done, or a simple encouraging phrase, "Nice try." If necessary, also discuss nonexamples (not nice talk) and have students provide their own examples.

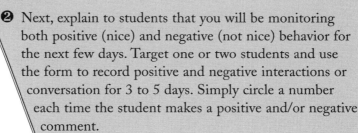

❷ Next, explain to students that you will be monitoring both positive (nice) and negative (not nice) behavior for the next few days. Target one or two students and use the form to record positive and negative interactions or conversation for 3 to 5 days. Simply circle a number each time the student makes a positive and/or negative comment.

❸ After the observation period, conference with the student and agree on a goal for improvement. The goal can reflect any of these measures of progress:
- an increase in positive comments,
- a decrease in negative comments, or
- a minimum number of positives or maximum number of negatives.

If you intend to use the form as part of a contract system, at this point you should also agree on a privilege, activity, or other reinforcer if the goal is met.

Note. This idea is adapted from *Interventions: Collaborative Planning for Students at Risk,* by R. Sprick, M. Sprick, and M. Garrison, 1993, Longmont, CO: Sopris West. Copyright 1993 by Sopris West. Adapted with permission.

❹ Once the goal has been set, observe and record for the next 5 to 10 school days. Some students can self-record, keeping track of their own progress.

❺ At the end of the contract period, conference with the student again and evaluate his or her progress. At this point, you can provide positive reinforcement, suggest a new target goal, and/or review ways of improving the student's performance.

Name _____   Date _____

Nice/Not Nice

Directions: Circle a number each time you say something nice or something not nice.

Date _____   Date _____

☺	☹
1	1
2	2
3	3
4	4
5	5
6	6
7	7
8	8
9	9
10	10
___	___

☺	☹
1	1
2	2
3	3
4	4
5	5
6	6
7	7
8	8
9	9
10	10
___	___

If you say nice things _____ times, you will get

Idea 20

Idea 21

I Spy Respect

Teachers of all students like to see respectful actions and talk in school. Since many students have backgrounds, expectations, and habits that are different from those of their teachers, "respect" may not mean the same thing to everyone. One way to help students learn how to demonstrate respect for themselves and others is to observe and record using the I Spy Respect procedure. This is an easy way to teach students desirable, positive, respectful behaviors while eliminating disrespectful talk and actions.

Here's how it works.

❶ First, construct a poster that has two columns. This is often called a T-chart because the paper can easily be divided by printing the letter "T." Label the left column of the paper Respectful and the right column Disrespectful.

❷ Throughout the week, keep a small pad of paper or some index cards available and clandestinely write down specific examples of respectful and disrespectful behaviors you witness. Try to be as discreet as possible, so students don't put on act when they think you are observing.

❸ At the end of each class period or day, record examples on the T-chart. Try to record a wide variety of specific comments and actions, so that students understand exactly what you mean.

❹ At the beginning of the next week, day, or class, discuss the examples with students. Explain exactly why you wrote each example in one of the two columns. When discussing disrespectful actions and comments, have students suggest some positive, viable alternatives.

Respectful

Thank you for the cookie.

I like you.

Would you like to play with me?

You're nice.

May I help you?

Disrespectful

Give me that!

You big stupid.

Get out of my way.

You can't play.

❺ After the initial observation period and teaching have been completed, ask students to set a goal regarding their behavior and let students select a privilege they would like to earn. For example, if students are observed making at least 10 positive comments from Monday until Thursday, then they get double recess on Friday.

❻ Use the next week to do more observations. At the end of the week, see if the class goal has been met. If so, it's reward time! If not, set a new goal and try again.

☞ **Tip:**

Try to focus on behavior all over the school, especially in the common areas like the halls, cafeteria, and outside. Many students have difficulty behaving respectfully in these less supervised and less structured areas.

Respectful	Disrespectful

Idea 21

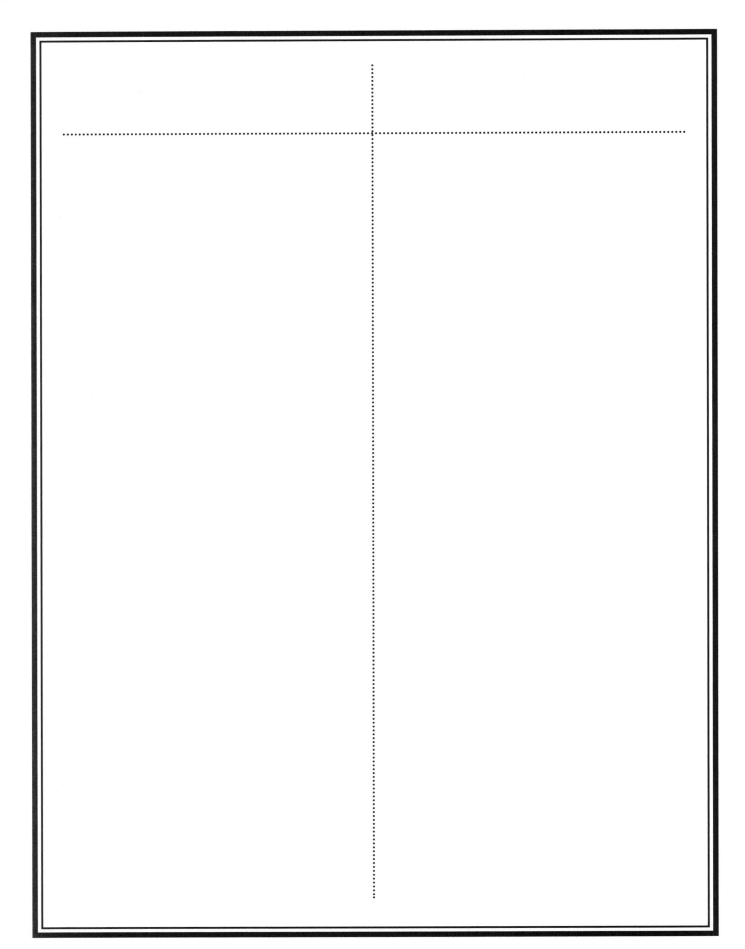

Idea 22
Hand Signs

When interacting with oppositional or challenging students, it is sometimes difficult to avoid getting pulled into arguments, explanations, discussions, and power struggles. In order to keep these unnecessary and unproductive exchanges to a minimum, you can use hand signs that work with all students. Here are some quick and easy nonverbal ways to signal students to stop talking and do what has been asked. It's a good idea to teach these signs to students before you use them, so there is no misunderstanding about their meanings. Hand signs are great because they are portable, quiet, visible from a distance, and easy to understand. Use them often!

**❶ Straight Arm Them
(a.k.a., Talk To My Hand)**

All you do here is extend your arm straight out, with your palm up and facing the student. The message here is to stop (and/or talk to my hand because I'm not listening.) Do not talk to the student while using this gesture.

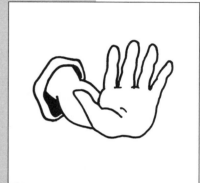

❷ Time Out

This sign is straight from sports and is almost universally understood. It involves putting one hand straight up, with fingers together, then placing the other hand flat across the top, so that the two hands together form the letter "T" (for "Time Out"). When students can't seem to stop themselves from going on and on, this signal is a great way to tell them they need to take a break. Students could also request a break by using this sign (with teacher permission).

❸ "No" in American Sign Language

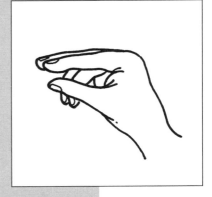

Saying "no" is often a difficult thing to do with students who are confrontational and/or intimidating. Sometimes, you might want to signal "no" instead of saying it verbally. This nonverbal communication also helps to avoid interruptions in instruction and arguments. The sign for "no" is a quick movement that brings together your thumb and two fingers into a closed position. It reminds us of a mouth closing quickly, which is probably a good analogy for students to learn.

❹ "Stop" in American Sign Language

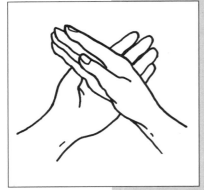

The sign for "Stop" is another good nonverbal word to teach your students. It uses both hands, both with open palms, fingers close together. Extend one hand out with palm up and "chop" it with the other, so that your hands cross each other to form a right angle. When the movement is done quickly and emphatically, the message to "stop" can be clearly understood.

❺ "Shhhhhhh"

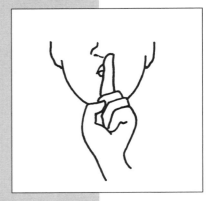

Parents, teachers, and librarians have used this sign for as long as we can remember. It is simple and easily understood. Just hold up your index finger in a vertical position, across your lips. Make eye contact and, if you need to, add a soft verbal "Shhhhhhh" to tell the student to be quiet. There should be no misunderstanding with this signal.

❻ Finger Counting

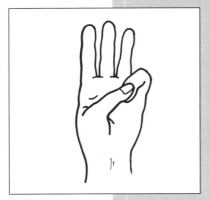

We have mentioned countdowns and cool downs several times in other ideas in the book. You can use your fingers to count either up or down with students for a variety of reasons. One system to teach your students is a 5-4-3-2-1 or 3-2-1 countdown. This can be used as a structured warning system by holding up one hand, fingers spread apart, then putting one finger down at a time. The message to the student is that he or she has 5 (or 3) chances, is being warned, and will face consequences if he or she has not followed directions by the time you get down to one finger (1).

Always make sure the consequences are clear before beginning a countdown, whether it uses fingers or number cards.

Idea 23
Take a Break

All students get upset and have problems from time to time. Although the problems are not always disruptive or serious, they can escalate and become more problematic if teachers fail to intervene. When students appear to be losing their composure or self-control, it is often helpful to give them a short break.

Educators and parents often use an intervention they call "time out." However, the term "time out" may mean something different to each individual who uses it. We like to differentiate two different types of intervention: one intended to give students an opportunity to regain composure and calm down and another used as a mild punishment for misbehavior. Take a Break helps students who are experiencing difficulty and need to calm down before they become disruptive or aggressive. It is not intended as punishment, but rather prevention.

To teach students how to calm down, try these steps.

❶ Find an area of the room that is away from traffic. Clear it of materials and activities, except for a small chair, study carrel, or floor mat.

❷ Explain to your students that this area will be available to them when they need a quiet place to calm down.

❸ Teach students a signal or phrase that you will use to indicate that they need to move to the break area. Also suggest that they learn a similar signal or phrase to indicate when they feel themselves losing composure or self-control. We have included some examples of signal cards that are helpful and you may also want to teach some simple gestures or hand signals. Use something simple like the "T" signal used to indicate a time out in football, formed with one hand vertical and the other across the top to make the lid of the "T."

❹ Give each student an opportunity to practice responding to your signal or making a request to move to the break area. Review the procedures regularly, explaining to students that the break area is not a punishment, but rather a place to regroup, reflect, and calm down.

❺ While students are sitting in the break area, suggest that they read the signs provided, which explain a sequence of suggestions to assist them relax and focus on behaving more appropriately. You may wish to set a timer for the student, from 1 minute to 5 minutes, depending on students' ages.

❻ After the student is calm and ready to return to the learning situation, praise and reinforce him or her, using the Great Break coupons as concrete reinforcement and a reminder of a job well done.

Take a Break

Idea 23

Take a Break

Idea 23

Take a Break	Time for a Break
Take a Break	Time for a Break
Take a Break	Time for a Break
Take a Break	Time for a Break

(Older Students)

Idea 23

I Need a Break	Give Me a Break
I Need a Break	Give Me a Break
I Need a Break	Give Me a Break
I Need a Break	Give Me a Break

(Older Students)

Idea 23

(Younger Students)

Idea 23

(Younger Students)

Idea 23

Take a Break

Sit quietly.

Breathe slowly.

Think of something nice.

Tell the teacher you are calm.

Great Break!

You did a great job getting calm.

You may _____

_____

You're So Cool!

For being so cool during your break, you get a chance to:

_____

Great Break!

You did a great job getting calm.

You may _____

_____

You're So Cool!

For being so cool during your break, you get a chance to:

_____

Great Break!

You did a great job getting calm.

You may _____

_____

You're So Cool!

For being so cool during your break, you get a chance to:

_____

Idea 23

Idea 24
Teach Students the "Three Bs"

Teachers frequently find themselves wishing that students would demonstrate self-control, especially when interacting with others around them. Actually teaching the self-control skills can be a challenge, however, since teachers have little time and few materials to provide them with ideas. Fortunately, there are some simple ways to teach self-control skills to students that require few materials at all. One example is the Three Bs. This is a cognitive-behavioral strategy. Teachers can teach a sequence in which students talk themselves through a situation without losing control.

Here's how to teach the Three Bs.

❶ Model for students by saying the steps aloud.

❷ Ask students to practice saying the steps aloud.

❸ Have students demonstrate the steps without actually talking.

❹ Set up scenarios or simulations, and ask students to demonstrate what they would do and how they would react.

❺ Provide students with corrective feedback and praise.

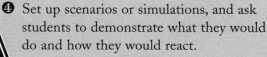

Three Bs

Be quiet
Back away
Breathe deeply

☞ **Tip:**

Students can carry the small, wallet-size reminder card so that they can practice repeating the Three Bs throughout the day.

Three Bs

Be quiet
To calm down, stop talking.

Back away
To keep from getting more upset, back away.

Breathe deeply
Take one or two deep breaths to release stress.

Three Bs

Be quiet

Back away

Breathe deeply

Three Bs

Be quiet

Back away

Breathe deeply

Three Bs

Be quiet

Back away

Breathe deeply

Three Bs

Be quiet

Back away

Breathe deeply

Idea 25
Copy the Rule

Occasionally, a student's behavior will escalate rapidly, turning a minor problem into a big behavioral crisis. This is often the case with students who are excitable, emotionally volatile, or impulsive. If you know that a student is becoming very upset and highly agitated, you can sometimes calm things down by by interrupting the behavior pattern.

One simple way to disrupt the student's momentum is to ask him or her to copy something. This task requires that the student sit and work on something simple that does not require a lot of thought or discussion. Copying encourages the student to focus on something other than the incident or event that originally caused the problem. Older students can copy classroom rules; younger students can copy letters or numbers. We have provided some simple patterns, but teachers can easily find similar tasks that involve a calm, routine activity designed to deescalate students' behavior.

Copy the Letters and Numbers

A   B   C   D   E   F

G   H   I   J   K   L

M   N   O   P   Q   R

S   T   U   V   W   X

Y   Z   1   2   3   4

5   6   7   8   9   10

Idea 25

Copy Time

1. _____

2. _____

3. _____

4. _____

5. _____

6. _____

Idea 25

Copy These Rules

When I am upset, I will use words instead of actions.

_____

_____

_____

_____

I will walk away from arguments.

_____

_____

_____

_____

When I am feeling tense, I will take two or three deep breaths.

_____

_____

_____

_____

Copy These Rules

Idea 25

Idea 26
Help Cards

Because there is always the potential for serious problems in classrooms, it is a good idea to be prepared for emergencies. When an emergency occurs, whether it is a medical problem, a confrontation between students, or a crisis involving an aggressive student, an effective system of communication should be established and functioning. Teachers who work in classrooms without telephones, intercoms, or beepers should teach their students an easy, effective method of requesting assistance, just in case they cannot leave the room themselves. Help Cards are a good option for teachers whose students have poor verbal communication skills, forget information when stressed, or just need some extra support.

Follow these steps.

❶ Copy the cards on heavy-duty yellow or red paper.

❷ Laminate the cards and put them in an accessible place in the classroom. (For example, hang the cards on a hook right by the door.)

❸ Teach your students what the cards say and where the cards can be found.

❹ Next, teach students a simple routine that includes some basic steps.
 • When they hear a signal or short phrase (Get help now. Take the red card.)
 • Remove the card from the hook.
 • Move quickly to a predetermined destination (the office, the room across the hall, the class next door, etc.).
 • Hand the card to an adult.

❺ Make sure that the office staff and your fellow teachers know what the cards mean and what to do when presented with one. (Send an administrator, call security, etc.)

❻ Make sure all students know the routine and rotate responsibility for taking the card.

☞ Tip:

Practice once a week at random times.

105

The cards are most helpful when a teacher has no support from an instructional assistant and/or lacks a more sophisticated system of communication. We have provided two different Help Cards, one that can be copied on yellow paper and used when assistance is needed but no immediate crisis exists, and another that should be reproduced on red paper and used for critical emergencies. When giving the direction to take the card and seek help, the teacher should clearly say "Yellow Card" or "Red Card" so students know which one to use.

☞ **Caution:**

Help Cards are not designed to take the place of a comprehensive crisis plan. Students must be taught other procedures that should be followed in cases where weapons are involved or when other special circumstances occur.

Send Help to Room _____

Immediately

Send Help to Room _____

Immediately

Idea 26

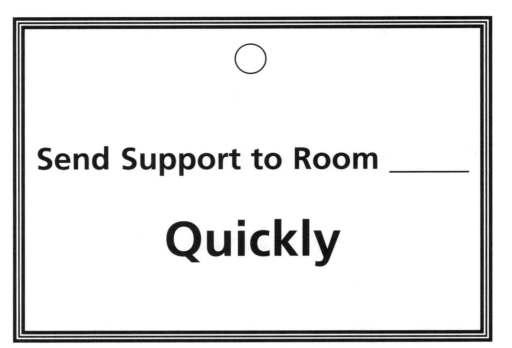

Send Support to Room _____

Quickly

Send Support to Room _____

Quickly

Idea 26

Idea 27

It Pays To Be Honest

Students who lie may experience some negative consequences from both peers and adults. After lying, other students may be less likely to trust them and adults may more closely scrutinize their actions and movements. We have provided a few strategies intended to reduce lying and increase telling the truth. (Icons provided in Appendix B.)

Here are some strategies to use.

❶ Try to be very direct when dealing with a student when you are absolutely sure he or she is lying. Stay calm and respond with a statement indicating that you are aware of the lie. Say something like, "I know that is not true. Let's move on to something else."

❷ Don't give too much attention to a student who lies often. Becoming overly agitated and upset may actually increase lying if the student lies in order to get attention.

❸ Don't wait until a student lies to focus on honesty. Praise and reward all students for telling the truth and being honest. We have included some raffle coupons that are a convenient way to encourage students to tell the truth, even in difficult situations or when admitting their fault or responsibility.

❹ If a student lies frequently and/or if the lies become harmful to others, dangerous, or reflective of highly negative feelings, call his or her parents in for a conference. If the student is old enough, you may want him or her to attend the conference as well. Provide the parents with specific information describing incidents when the student has lied. Ask for their input regarding solutions and interventions that can be carried out both at home and at school. If everyone agrees, write a contract that rewards honest behavior. The coupons can be part of your contract system.

You're Hot! A lie's not!  This is for being honest.	For telling the truth, you have earned _____ _____ _____
You're Hot! A lie's not!  This is for being honest.	For telling the truth, you have earned _____ _____ _____
You're Hot! A lie's not!  This is for being honest.	For telling the truth, you have earned _____ _____ _____
You're Hot! A lie's not! This is for being honest.	For telling the truth, you have earned _____ _____ _____

Idea 27

Idea 28
Stop, Think, and Choose

Teachers are always interested in teaching students to stop and think about what they are going to do. Having this set of skills in place often allows students to make better decisions. This particular technique can be used in a variety of common situations (e.g., cursing) and also with very specialized situations (e.g., cheating). The idea can be taught to one or more students. The basic elements of the idea are based on the principles of cognitive behavior modification and require instruction and practice.

Here's how it works.

❶ Develop a set of lessons that are designed to increase a student's self-regulatory behaviors.

❷ Have the students identify behaviors that have gotten them into trouble previously—or might in the future.

❸ Use the form as a vehicle for helping students generate choices for any behaviors that they have identified.

❹ If this idea is used in a group format, the group responses can be generated for some behaviors. In addition, other members in a group can comment on a particular student's choices.

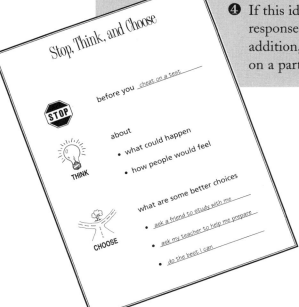

Stop, Think, and Choose

STOP

before you _____

THINK

about

- what could happen

- how people would feel

CHOOSE

what are some better choices

- _____

- _____

- _____

Idea 29
How It Feels

Many teachers impose punitive remedies on the child who steals or destroys other people's property. A preferable technique to deal with stealing involves a more positive perspective by getting the student to feel empathy for the other student who has been or will be offended by the act of stealing. The idea described below can be used with a student who is guilty of stealing/destroying others' property or can be used in a preventative way in a small group or with an entire class. This latter option involves having students think about the behavior and its effect on any potential victim.

Here is How It Feels works.

❶ Determine the purpose of why you will be discussing the issue of stealing—to remedy a problem that exists with a student or group of students or to prevent this behavior from occurring.

❷ Discuss the ramifications that stealing or vandalism has on others.

❸ Use the form as a way to get the student to think about how one's feelings can be hurt when someone steals or destroys a personal item.

❹ Make sure that the last part of the form is completed, as this is how the student can begin to think about various natural solutions to the problem. Note that the teacher should help the child generate options if he or she has problems doing so.

How It Feels

Draw a picture of your favorite possession.

How would you feel if someone took or destroyed it?

Draw a picture of what would make you feel better.

Idea 29

Idea 30
Positive Talk

When students are pessimistic, negative, or chronically unhappy, adults are often concerned about their emotional well being. When these same feelings are obvious to their peers, students may also be less likely to form and maintain friendships and close relationships. Being friends with someone who is always miserable can be exhausting and unpleasant instead of fun and invigorating. The challenge for educators is to develop some effective ways of increasing students' optimism and positive spirits that are not too time consuming or difficult to implement.

Here is one strategy that may work for students. It is a version of cognitive behavior modification, which teaches students to "talk themselves through" difficult situations. Teachers teach positive statements and responses through modeling and instruction, and then students imitate, practice, and cue themselves.

Here's how it works.

❶ Model for students both positive and negative comments. You can begin the discussion, then ask them to contribute their ideas. Discuss with them the important differences between positive and negative comments as well as the effect of each attitude on ourselves and others. Use the Positive Talk T-chart and the Let's Hear It chart to list examples that your students can understand.

❷ Suggest to students that they use the Positive Talk Cue Cards as a reminder to be positive. You may also decide to implement a contract that rewards your students for making positive, optimistic statements.

☞ **Tip:**

When beginning instruction, use an overhead of the T-chart to discuss examples.

Positive Talk T-Chart

Positive Comments	Negative Comments

Idea 30

Positive Talk

Let's Hear It

If this happens	☹ Instead of saying something negative like	☺ Say something positive like

Idea 30

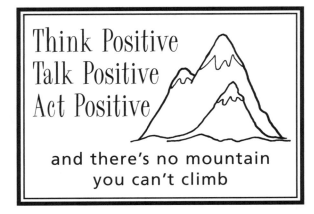

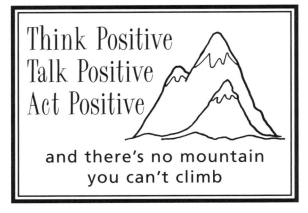

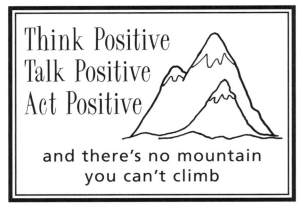

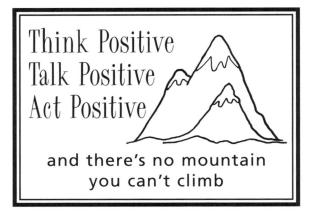

Idea 30

Idea 31
Games for the Group

When you want to have fun with the entire class, games can be just what you need. Here are five enjoyable games to play with your students. These games have some qualities that classroom teachers really appreciate:

- Students don't move around a lot. This helps prevent behavior problems with students who like to push and shove.

- All five games are easy to play and don't require much in the way of equipment or supplies.

- In the case of Silent Speedball, there is no talking allowed. This keeps noise to a minimum and prevents arguing and accusations.

❶ **Silent Speedball**

Students stand by their desks or in a large circle. Without talking, they quickly throw a soft Nerf ball to each other. When students fail to catch the ball, they must sit down. The last person standing wins the game. Randomly assign a student "judge" to decide if the miss was due to a bad throw. If so, the catcher remains in the game.

❷ **Seven-Up**

Seven students line up at the front of the room. Seated students put their heads down on their desks and hold up one thumb in the "thumbs up" position. Without talking, each of the Seven-Up students chooses one seated student by pressing their thumbs down gently. Once all the Seven-Up choose and are lined up back at the front, the teacher says, "heads up."

Chosen students stand and one-by-one guess who chose them (one guess only). If they are correct, they take their chooser's place, otherwise they sit down.

119

❸ Balloon Ball

Students form two teams and sit side-by-side in chairs that are arranged in two long rows about 6 feet across from and facing each other. Each student has a baton made of a rolled-up section of newspaper, taped together, about 10 to 12 inches long. The teacher blows up two large balloons and hits them into the air, one at each end of the rows. Without getting out of their chairs, students hit the balloons back and forth. If a balloon lands on the floor behind a row, the opposite team gets a point. Play until a team gets 10 or 15 points.

❹ Catch the Candy

The teacher sets a timer and very quickly throws pieces of candy (underhand; not too hard or fast) to students. Students catch as many pieces as they can in the allotted amount of time (3 to 5 minutes). Keep a basket or jar handy and filled with a variety of types of candy. Let the hero help with the throwing.

❺ Simon Says

Students stand by desks or in a large circle. One student or the teacher is Simon. Simon gives directions (e.g., touch your nose with your index finger). Students must follow directions beginning with the words "Simon says." Students must not follow directions not beginning with "Simon says." Students who follow the direction anyway sit down. The last person standing becomes the new Simon.

Idea 32

Color On Cards

Stores and catalogues often use "scratch off" cards to provide discounts to customers. Just like the scratch offs used in lotteries, these cards are motivating because customers never know what they might win, but have great hopes for possibly winning a big prize or getting a huge discount. Color On Cards take advantage of the same key factors to motivate students: chance and hope. You will need a set of color changing markers, some heavy-duty paper, and ideas for ways to make the cards exciting.

Here's how the Color On Cards work.

❶ Photocopy the card masters onto heavy stock paper. You can use the masters provided here or make up your own and print color copies from your computer.

❷ After copying and cutting out the cards, use a white, invisible ink marker to write a number that indicates the amount of discount, a number for extra points, the minutes of special activity time, or a drawing that represents other positive reinforcement.

❸ Put the cards into envelopes and seal them or put them face down in a stack. Students should not be able to see what is written with the invisible ink.

❹ When a student meets his or her goal or your criterion, he or she picks a card from the stack or chooses an envelope. It's a good idea to make this a special occasion. (Think drum rolls, a big ceremony, a special class meeting, and so on.)

❺ Using one of the colored markers, the student can then color over the invisible writing or drawing. A number or picture will "magically" appear.

❻ Make sure you provide the reward as quickly as possible.

You have earned 15 minutes of talk time.

Here are some examples of behaviors that teachers can reinforce with Color On Cards.

- Students earn _____ minutes of art time for finishing their work in class.

- Students earn _____ bonus points on their behavior sheets for ignoring the misbehavior of others.

- Students can earn _____ minutes of board game time if they turn in completed homework on time.

- Students earn _____ minutes of computer game time.

- A student gets to sit by a friend for _____ minutes.

Resources for Color Changing Markers

www.pentechintl.com
www.kpwtoys.com
www.pfot.com
www.vanker.com

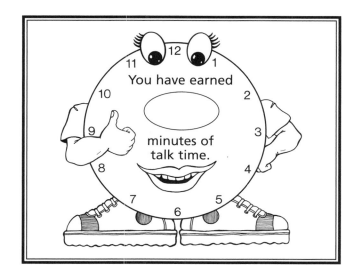

You have earned

_____

minutes of talk time.

Computer time is yours.

You have earned

_____

minutes because you

_____

_____

_____

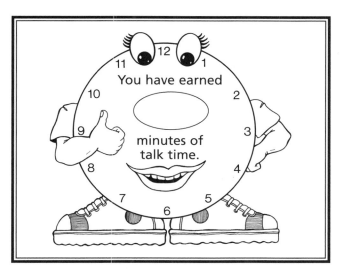

You have earned

_____

minutes of talk time.

Computer time is yours.

You have earned

_____

minutes because you

_____

_____

_____

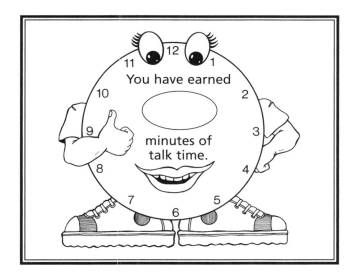

You have earned

_____

minutes of talk time.

Computer time is yours.

You have earned

_____

minutes because you

_____

_____

_____

Idea 32

Free Reading Time

Color the spot to see how many minutes of free reading time you have earned.

Art time is yours.

Take ⬭ minutes.

Free Reading Time

Color the spot to see how many minutes of free reading time you have earned.

Art time is yours.

Take ⬭ minutes.

Free Reading Time

Color the spot to see how many minutes of free reading time you have earned.

Art time is yours.

Take ⬭ minutes.

Idea 32

Idea 33

Here's Your Menu

We recognize the important role that high quality instruction, challenging and exciting lessons, positive relationships with adults, meaningful learning experiences, and ongoing success play in encouraging students to work hard and do well. There is no doubt that teachers can and do have an important effect on students' success in school and it would be great if all students were intrinsically motivated to achieve at their potential. Unfortunately, this ideal situation does not exist in all classrooms. Even the best teachers often face students who are not intrinsically motivated.

While the long-term goal may be to discontinue these "extrinsics," some students occasionally require some motivating events, privileges, and tangible items. Because it is sometimes tricky to figure out exactly what each individual student values or wants, it is helpful to offer a menu of positive reinforcers. The positive reinforcement menus presented here (for groups and individuals) are examples that teachers can easily replicate and change. We advise you to do just that—use these examples as a beginning, but do not hesitate to expand, vary, modify, update, and improve on our idea. Students will love the variety and novelty, as well as your creative spirit. (Icons provided in Appendix B.)

Note. This idea is adapted from *Practical Ideas That Really Work for Students with ADHD,* by K. McConnell, G. Ryser, and J. Higgins, 2000, Austin, TX: PRO-ED, Inc. Copyright 2000 by PRO-ED, Inc. Adapted with permission.

This Is Your Menu

❑   Clean off the overheads

❑   Wipe the board

❑   Run errands today

❑   Listen to music or a story on tape

❑   Have lunch with your favorite teacher

❑   Water the plants

❑   A good note to take home

❑   Free video rental coupon

❑   Read a book or magazine alone

❑   Go to the library

❑   Extra computer time

❑   You pick your pen (colored ink, pencil, marker)

Idea 33

Here's Your Class Menu

❑   Talk time

❑   Ice cream treat or soda at the end of the day

❑   Read aloud time for the whole class

❑   Extra recess or break time for the whole class

❑   Talk time at the end of class

❑   Have class outside during nice weather

❑   Popcorn or candy for everyone

❑   Game time for 15 minutes

❑   Lunch in the room; teacher makes dessert

❑   "Good note" home for everyone

❑   Music during work time

❑   New pencil or pen for everyone

Idea 33

This Is Your Menu

☐ _____

☐ _____

☐ _____

☐ _____

☐ _____

☐ _____

☐ _____

☐ _____

☐ _____

☐ _____

☐ _____

☐ _____

Idea 33

Daily Specials

Story

Teacher reads story

Pizza

Have a class pizza party

Recess

Get 10 extra minutes of recess time

Snacks

Teacher provides a snack for the class

_____

_____

Idea 33

Idea 34

Forms for You

While it is often possible to effectively use group management techniques to improve students' behavior, some students may need a more individualized approach. To help teachers monitor and track individual student's behaviors, evaluation and feedback forms are often very useful. In this section, we have provided some tools to help you as you focus on individual students and/or individual behaviors. This section includes several forms for observation, tracking, daily reporting, feedback, and contracting. Most are very simple to use and directions have been provided. (Icons provided in Appendix B.)

Directions

One at a Time

This form gives teachers a tool for observing one target behavior at time. To use the form, first identify and describe the target behavior at the top of the form. Next, place photographs, icons, picture symbols, or drawings in the left column. Each visual representation should indicate a period of time during which the student will be observed. Generally, children who are in preschool should be observed during 5 to 10 minute intervals. Students in kindergarten through second or third grade will often require feedback after about 10 to 20 minutes. In the right column on the form there are two smiley face symbols, representing acceptable or unacceptable performance on the target behavior. At the end of the observation period, the teacher should circle the face corresponding to the student's level of performance. At the same time, it is very important that the teacher give the student enthusiastic praise for demonstrating the target behavior and corrective feedback if the behavior was not observed. The bottom section of the form can be used as a contract with the student, so that the child can select a choice of positive reinforcement options if his or her goal is met.

☞ **Tip:**

If a behavior is very disruptive and/or occurring very frequently, shorten the observation time intervals. With young children, it is important to vary the reinforcers often.

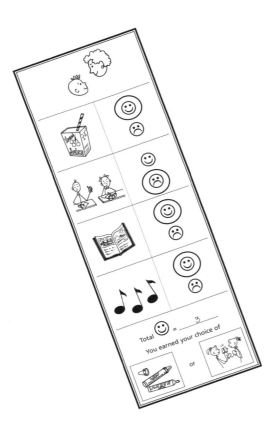

Total 😊 = _____

You earned your choice of

or

Total 😊 = _____

You earned your choice of

or

Countoon Contract

Discuss with the student a problem behavior that needs to change. Set a criterion slightly above or below current performance, depending on whether you would like to reduce or increase the frequency of the behavior. (For example, if Sally is calling out 10 times, set her criterion at 8. If Gino is only volunteering in class twice per week, set the criterion at four times per week.) Ask the student to select a reinforcer that he or she would like to earn if the criterion is met. To create the countoon, circle the criterion then put a picture of the behavior in the first panel and a picture of the reward in the third panel. Teach the student to self-record his or her behavior by crossing through consecutive numbers each time he or she demonstrates the behavior. Do a couple of practice sessions in which both the teacher and student monitor, then compare the two recordings. Either place the countoon permanently on the student's desk, or if using regular copies, use one per day or class period. Once the student meets the criterion, immediately provide the reinforcer.

Note. The Countoon Contract is from *Practical Ideas That Really Work for Students with ADHD*, by K. McConnell, G. Ryser, and J. Higgins, 1999, Austin, TX: PRO-ED, Inc. Copyright 1999 by PRO-ED, Inc. Reprinted with permission.

Countoon Contract

What I Do	How Many	What I Get
	1 2 3 4 5 6 7 8 9 10 11 12	

Idea 34

Make Me Smile

Write three simple rules (e.g., stay in area; raise hand; say something nice). If a rule is broken, cross off a smiley face and write the rule number in the blank to the side. If at least one smiley face is left each day, the student earns points or tickets.

Note. Make Me Smile is from *Practical Ideas That Really Work for Students with ADHD*, by K. McConnell, G. Ryser, and J. Higgins, 1999, Austin, TX: PRO-ED, Inc. Copyright 1999 by PRO-ED, Inc. Reprinted with permission. The Make Me Smile idea provided by and used with permission of Angela Burns, third-grade teacher, Pine Tree Intermediate School, Longview, Texas.

Make Me Smile

Rules

1 _____

2 _____

3 _____

Mon.   ☺ ☺ ☺   ___ ___ ___
Tues. ☺ ☺ ☺   ___ ___ ___
Wed.   ☺ ☺ ☺   ___ ___ ___
Thurs. ☺ ☺ ☺   ___ ___ ___
Fri.   ☺ ☺ ☺   ___ ___ ___

Student Signature

Make Me Smile

Rules

1 _____

2 _____

3 _____

Mon.   ☺ ☺ ☺   ___ ___ ___
Tues. ☺ ☺ ☺   ___ ___ ___
Wed.   ☺ ☺ ☺   ___ ___ ___
Thurs. ☺ ☺ ☺   ___ ___ ___
Fri.   ☺ ☺ ☺   ___ ___ ___

Student Signature

Idea 34

Card Counters

Card Counters are a great way to ensure positive reinforcement that is concrete, visual, and easy to manage. The samples provided here can be used to record and reinforce students each time they demonstrate a target behavior. Set a goal with the student, then punch with a hole punch, color in with a marker, cover the holes with small stickers, or make a line after each occurrence of the target behavior. Students enjoy seeing their progress, and you have a simple management and reinforcement system.

Note. The Card Counters are from *Practical Ideas That Really Work for Students with Autism Spectrum Disorders*, by K. McConnell and G. Ryser, 2000, Austin, TX: PRO-ED, Inc. Copyright 2000 by PRO-ED, Inc. Reprinted with permission. They were originally adapted from *Practical Ideas That Really Work for Students with ADHD*, by K. McConnell, G. Ryser, and J. Higgins, 1999, Austin, TX: PRO-ED, Inc. Copyright 1999 by PRO-ED, Inc. Adapted with permission.

When you _____ we'll punch your card.

Target Behavior

When the card is all punched out, you have earned _____.

Reinforcer

When you _____ we'll color your card.

Target Behavior

When the card is all colored, you have earned _____.

Reinforcer

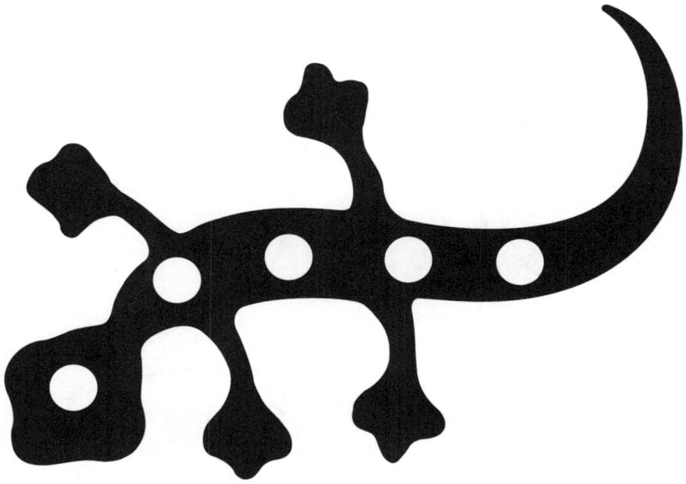

When you _____ we'll draw a line on your card.

Target Behavior

When all of the lines are drawn, you have earned _____.

Reinforcer

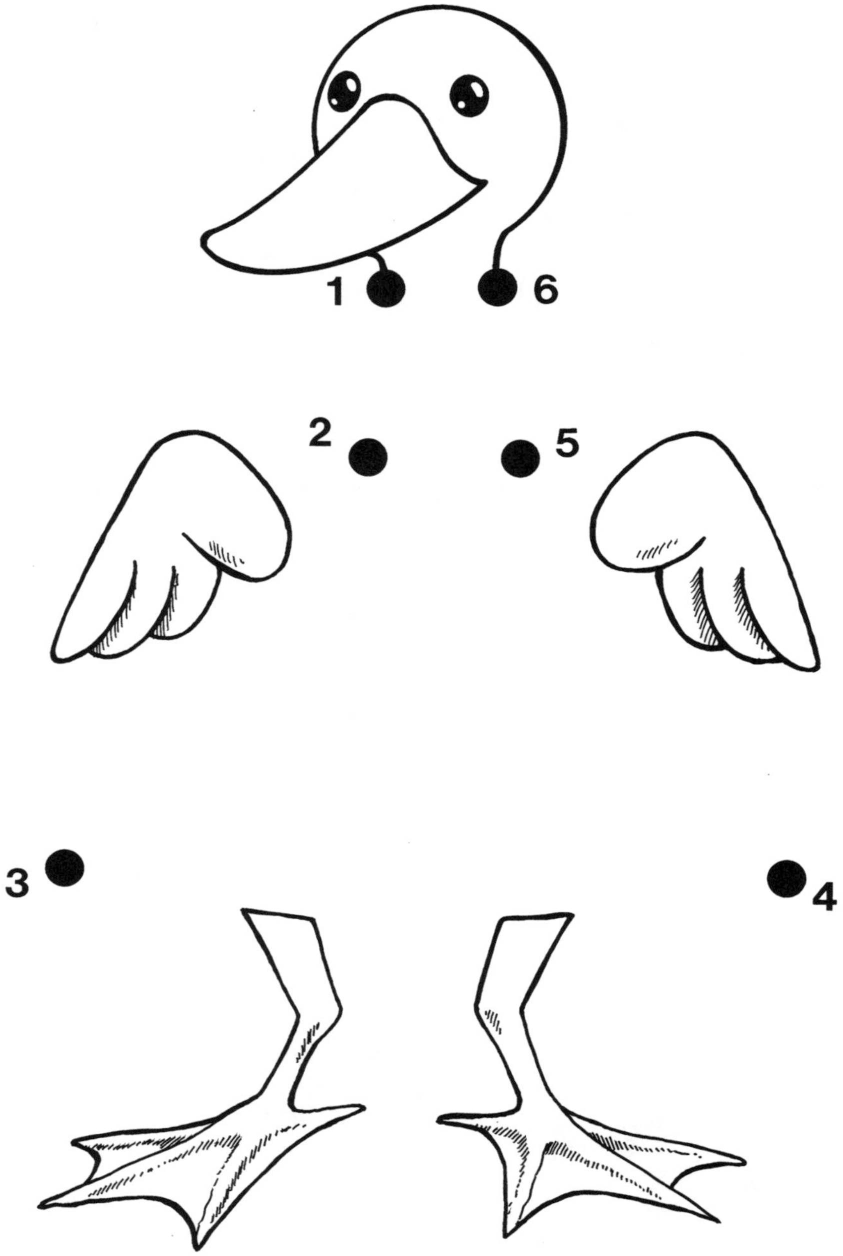

1 ● ● 6

2 ● ● 5

3 ● ● 4

Positive Behavior Contract. Choose two basic target behaviors and two reinforcers. Indicate the goals to students by using pictures or symbols that represent the behaviors and reinforcers selected. Fill in the time intervals, circle the faces, and reinforce if the behavior has been on target.

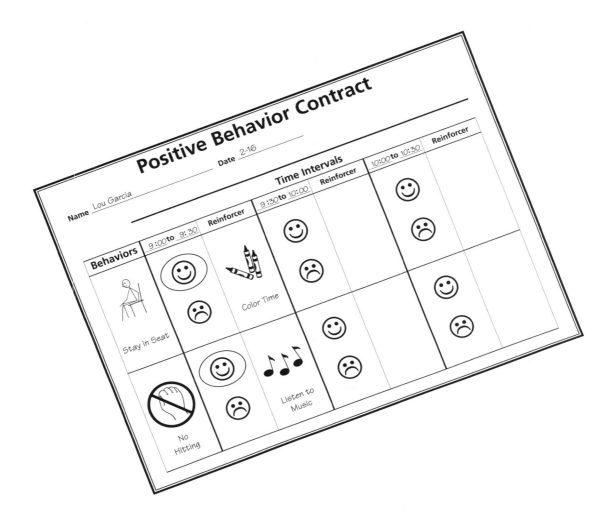

Note. The Positive Behavior Contract is from *Practical Ideas That Really Work for Students with Autism Spectrum Disorders*, by K. McConnell and G. Ryser, 2000, Austin, TX: PRO-ED, Inc. Copyright 2000 by PRO-ED, Inc. Reprinted with permission.

Positive Behavior Contract

Name _____ Date _____

Time Intervals

Behaviors	: ___ to ___ :	Reinforcer	: ___ to ___ :	Reinforcer	: ___ to ___ :	Reinforcer
	:) :(		:) :(		:) :(	
	:) :(		:) :(		:) :(	

Idea 34

Appendix A
Intervention Plan Blackline Master

Student _____ Date _____

Teacher _____

Intervention Plan

BEHAVIOR	INTERVENTION IDEA NUMBER	START DATE	NOTES
_____	_____	_____	_____
	_____		_____
_____	_____	_____	_____
	_____		_____
_____	_____	_____	_____
	_____		_____
_____	_____	_____	_____
	_____		_____
_____	_____	_____	_____
	_____		_____
_____	_____	_____	_____
	_____		_____
_____	_____	_____	_____
	_____		_____
_____	_____	_____	_____
	_____		_____
_____	_____	_____	_____
	_____		_____
_____	_____	_____	_____
	_____		_____

Appendix B
Icon Blackline Masters

Positive Behaviors

raise hand

stay in seat

eyes on own work

prepared

say nice things

try hard

finish work

help others

compliant with teacher

smile

keep hands to self

stay focused on work

Negative Behaviors

talking out

leaving seat

eyes not on own work

not prepared

say mean things

not trying

unfinished work

not helping others

noncompliant with teacher

frown

hands not to self

not focused on work

Reinforcers

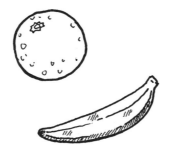

| pizza party | fruit | raisins |

| cookie | chips | popcorn |

| juice drink | lunch with a teacher | markers |

| reading time | music | computer time |

Reinforcers

play game with a friend

extra recess

talk time